JERRI

J E R R I

A Black Woman's Life in the Media

Jerri Lange

This book was printed in the United States of America.

Please address all inquires to Ishmael Reed Publishing Co.

P.O. Box 3288

Berkeley, CA 94703

To order additional copies of this book, contact:

Xlibris Corporation

1-888-795-4274

www.Xlibris.com

Orders@Xlibris.com

26390

Contents

Dedication

To my parents, Laura and Turner Wilson
My sons, Ted, Michael and James
And to my grandsons, Ted IV and Turner

INTRODUCTION

I first met Jerri Lange in 1964 when she walked into the office of the executive editor of the *San Francisco Chronicle*.

She had entered the oaken portals of this weather-stained gothic battlement at Fifth and Mission streets for her first day at work in the newspaper business. She took the elevator to the third floor, knocked pensively on the frosted glass door of the executive editor's office, then crossed the threshold into her brave new world.

Her new duties, in addition to becoming my secretary, included Girl Friday and secretary to satirist and national columnist Arthur Hoppe; Count Marco, the dandy adviser to lovelorn women and Charles McCabe, a Scotch whisky tosspot who could write about inconsiderable subjects—including his own divorces—more beautifully than any other newspaperman on earth.

There is no point in detailing Jerri's remarkable career. She tells the story so much better herself. It is a straightforward, touching saga of a little girl who simply refused to grow old, or bitter, during her trip through life. At times a lesser spirit might have turned sour, but Jerri has ever been a kind of dignified blithe spirit.

Jerri is a very rare person. She is a genuine San Francisco landmark, a bona fide paid up member of the exclusive club of San Francisco regulars. She is respected and loved by all those friends she met during her passage from Oakland to her future endeavors.

Jerri Lange

This writer can never forget the winsome young lady who walked into his office so many years ago, with just a touch of panic in her eyes. Her story is a little island of serenity in a world that has gone half crazy.

Scott Newhall, Executive Editor
San Francisco Chronicle

PREFACE

Jerri—A Black Woman's Life in the Media—is a case example in putting incredibly powerful—even culture-changing thoughts into simple sentences.

It is clear that Jerri Lange came of a family rich in love for individuals and for the American process of development and living. It is equally clear that she is nourished by the American thought of being independent and promoting the welfare of all society rather than living off of it with excuses for a non-productive life. Her philosophy is simple: Do the best you can with any opportunity that appears, and don't forget to work hard to prepare yourself to be ready when it comes.

Years beyond the age for college she learned new skills. She used those skills to blossom into a world of power and knowledge as its freshest flower. She came to know some of the most powerful men of our day, and worked closely with genius writers until she absorbed some of their talent.

She mastered the craft. She suffered all the rebuffs and rejections without losing her ability to laugh, and to make her sentences sharp javelins of love, penetrating deep, and full of emotion and wisdom. She learned to attack and destroy cozy ideas of status-quo without anger. She manages her style of writing, to include her learned perspective on the total culture, and on her time and place in that culture.

Jerri Lange goes further. Each thought seems to rise with special meaning, like the smoke signal of her ancestors. Those gifted and sensitive ones who can read the added message, see in the subtle rings: Those who love America speak the dialect of the heart: Love and happiness will win and be a joy forever.

Eugene E. Whitworth, Ph.D D.OJS, D. Tao. Dr. Whitworth is an instructor of writing. He has been awarded a coveted Bharat Ratna (Jewel of India) elected Poet Laureate of Tarma Province, and authored plays, musicals, poetry and many novels.

"We assume that our familiar senses give us a complete picture of our environment, but nothing could be further from the truth. We are stone-deaf and color-blind in a universe of impressions beyond the range of our senses."

Arthur C. Clark
Profiles of the Future, 1967
Henry Holt & Co., Publisher

FOREWORD

When I was a young girl growing up in Berkeley, we lived in a house on Ashby Avenue, near San Pablo Avenue. It was quite a busy intersection for such a small town. We used to play a wonderful game called Hide and Seek. We had to hide and make it back before being found. Each player had to yell a freedom call if we made it back.

Early one evening, while hiding from the gang, and with the echo of 'olly, olly, oxen free' ringing in my ears, I ran to hide in a place I had never been before, and chanced to notice a little thatched roof hut, where a lot of activity seemed to be going on. I peered out from behind the bush, and stood transfixed as I watched women in long, elegant gowns, accompanied by gentlemen dressed in black tie, emerge from large automobiles, with doors being opened for them by white-coated attendants. They were entering the hut, over which hung a sign that said "Hinky Dink's." I wondered what on earth they were doing there; I seemed to be viewing life from another planet, not the other side of town. I was getting a look at the good life, part of the American Dream. What I didn't realize at the time was that piece of the Dream was never intended for me. Thank God no one ever told me that or I would never have written this book.

Many years later, as a member of the Board of Directors of the Oakland Symphony, I attended a post-dinner party at Trader Vic's, the last such event before it moved to its new Watergate Restaurant. Accompanied by my son, Michael, our car drove up to the front of the restaurant; the door of our car swung open, and I was greeted by a white-coated attendant. As I stepped from the car it suddenly dawned on me where I was. I looked over to the left and there it was, that same old bush, much larger now but still standing and looking strangely familiar. Hinky Dink's had become Trader Vic's!

Time seemed to stop. Slowly I began to see the image of a young, skinny-legged, Black girl hiding behind the bush, her two bushy pigtails protruding from either side, staring out at the events taking place on that strange evening so long ago.

Only this time she was smiling, because the woman I was looking at was me! There are all kinds of illusions, from a little girl wanting to be part of a beautiful world she had never seen, to a little boy dreaming of flying into space.

Until the events of September 11, 2001, what was happening around the world seemed irrelevant to most Americans. As long as it did not affect the stock market or our daily lives, it did not register on our radar. We live inside a cocoon of comfort that fails to see the pain and suffering of others, even those in our midst.

This book begins with the story of my life as a Black woman in America, similar to millions of other Black women in this country. You won't find us on the news, because "if you're Black and not in trouble, you're not news." You won't find us on any sitcoms either. You have to be larger than life to make that cut. So if we live our lives without incident, raise our children, pay our taxes and contribute to society as best we can, you may never know us at all. We have been living below your radar for almost three hundred years. Your view of us is what you read in the newspapers, watch on television, or see in the movies. Television is the medium through which we can begin to understand each other. We need to break out of the little boxes created for us by a mass media determined to keep people in their place. (They are so much easier to control!) But events are happening so fast around us that we no longer have the luxury of not knowing our neighbors. The world has become a dangerous place, where not knowing your neighbor can cost your life. If September 11 taught us anything, it should be that reaching out and trying to understand another point of view is a good starting place on the road to the freedom and democracy we keep declaring our allegiance to.

J e r r i

Television can not solve all the problems, but it can begin the dialogue.

*   *   *

In my career as a broadcaster I would meet and interview many different people, from military generals to Hollywood stars, from the radical left to the conservative right, and travel half-way around the world to the wedding of a King. My world would always be one of conflict, bridging two worlds, one Black and one White.

The mythology of contrast between light and dark, night and day, yin and yang, good and evil, reaches its apex in the lives of those born Black who must live in a White world. Like the flight of the Phoenix, each time a match is put to our dreams, we must rise from the ashes. With each rising, there are bitter pills to swallow and lessons to be learned.

But somehow, that's true of us all, for we all stand before the door of Time at that very special moment, when we wait to enter a new place, listen to a different drummer or experience another world. I bid you, open this door and enter mine.

PART I

FAMILY

LAURA MCKEE COWAN, Grandmother. Born in New Orleans, Louisiana. Came to Oakland, California-post Civil War. Photo date unknown.

LAURA COWAN WILSON, Mother. Born in Oakland, California. Married and had 4 children, Lorraine, Stanley, Geraldine and Phyllis. Photo taken by Bill Batchan, 1954.

FAMILY

TURNER WILSON, Father. Born Anniston, Alabama. Buffalo Soldier. Served under General "Black Jack" Pershing; discharged from service at San Francisco Presidio, 1906, just weeks before the San Francisco Earthquake. Settled in Oakland. Photograph taken early 1900s, in New York City.

PHYLLIS ANDERSON, Sister. Born in Oakland. Photograph by Olan Mills, 1992.

FAMILY

STAN WILSON, Brother. Born in Oakland. Folksinger, Hungry I, San Francisco. Photo taken 1950, in San Francisco.

TED LANGE, JR., Husband of Jerri Lange. Born in New Orleans, Louisiana. Family photo, 1942.

FAMILY

TED LANGE III, Eldest son. Best known for his role as Isaac Washington on the ABC series "LOVEBOAT." Photo by Jane Hunt, 1992.

MICHAEL LANGE. Re-creates the role of Malcolm X and his best known speeches. Photo by Jonathan Eubanks, 2000.

FAMILY

JAMES COWAN. Oakland businessman. Family photo, 1994.

EARLY EMPLOYMENT

SCOTT NEWHALL, Executive Editor, San Francisco Chronicle. S.F. Chronicle Photograph, 1968.

FAMILY

Mayor John F. Shelley and Staff, San Francisco City Hall, 1967.
Photo courtesy of the Mayor's Office.

Lecture to Graduate Communications Class—Redwood Hall, Stanford
University-(Bill Rivers, Professor). Photo by Ted Kurihara, 1970.

Jerri Returns to Berkeley High School in 1974. Photo courtesy of
Ted Kurihara.

CHAPTER I

THE EARLY YEARS

Our family history begins around 1820 in the Southern town of Anniston, Alabama. It was there that many escaped slaves found their way to refuge with Indian tribes. They inter-married, learned the Indian way of survival, lived closer to nature and raised their families. On my father's side, my grandfather was one of those escaped slaves; my grandmother was a Seminole Indian.

Most of the Indian tribal lands scattered throughout the South became places where escaping slaves could disappear. All over the South, these tribes rescued Black slaves who were running from White masters. Today you will find millions of Blacks with Indian blood running through their veins.

The Seminole Indian tribe was especially unique because it was the only tribe never captured or put on a reservation. The Seminoles were fiercely protective of their wives. Their leader was a fierce warrior called Osceola, who evaded capture until his wives were kidnapped and held on a nearby military base. When Osceola went to negotiate the release of his wives, carrying a white flag, he was captured and placed under house arrest. He died in 1838 at Ft. Moultrie.

The Seminoles risked their lives to live in the Okefenokee swamps of Florida-with alligators and poisonous snakes—rather than live on reservations.

The children of the marriages of escaped Africans and recalcitrant Indians were a special breed—there was no memory of long term captivity in their blood. They had risked lives and limbs for freedom. Although they came from different cultures, they had much in common. They could not live under domination of the White man.

My father, Turner Wilson, was the son of a full-blooded Seminole Indian mother, and his father was a runaway slave. Our Indian family name was Snow. The Seminoles were a mixture of Creek Indians and Blacks through intermarriage. No wonder none of us would ever be comfortable on a plantation, be it the classic one in the South, or the many forms it would take in the North. We were all loners; it ran deep in our blood and in the blood of our ancestors. Some of these families relocated in other states. My father's family settled in Alabama. One day when my grandfather was away and my grandmother was at home with the children, two White men entered the house and started to rape her. My father remembered her saying, "Please, not in front of the children." They put gunny sacks over the head of each child and continued with the assault.

My father never got over the incident, and later ran away from home at the age of fourteen. I believe he ran to other relatives he knew by the name of Wilson, and was subsequently adopted by them. This part of his life was sketchy and he rarely discussed it with us.

He always started his story with his trek to the North. After staying with his new family for a while, he had decided to join the army. He felt his chances would be better if he joined up in the North. On the train he sat in the Jim Crow section with other Blacks. The trouble started when they hit the Mason Dixon Line. The conductor came into the car and announced that all the Black people had to come up and sit in the front car. My father didn't realize what was happening until he was ushered into a car with all White people. Terrified, he broke from the conductor and ran back to the Jim Crow car where he felt safe. The conductor came after him and escorted him back into the car up front, assuring him no one would hurt him. This was my father's introduction to the North and speaks to the severe impact of Southern brutality toward Blacks at that time. The fact that my father felt unsafe on a train, even though he was headed north, seems almost ludicrous now. He put his age up to 16 (which was easy at the time since there were no birth certificates of slaves or their children), and joined the Army, which became part of the 10th Cavalry that fought in the Spanish-American War, and charged San Juan Hill with Teddy Roosevelt. He was honorably discharged from the San Francisco Presidio in 1906 just before the San Francisco earthquake.

On my mother's side, my grandmother was Laura McKee Cowan, an octoroon from New Orleans. Octoroon meant you had four different bloods. In my grandmother's veins ran African, French, Spanish and Irish. She could "sit" on her hair, which was a sign of beauty in those days. I knew little of my grandfather, Ewing Cowan, except that he was Mulatto, a fact we discovered when a family member was tracing our roots in New Orleans. My mother was a member of the Cowan clan, daughter of Laura and Ewing Cowan who came to California from New Orleans just after the Civil War. Her brothers and sisters had wonderful old names like: Orinda, Florence, Mae; (my mother's twin sister), Aubrey, Homer, Percy and Delbert. Mama's parents died when she was just 14 years old, just nine months apart, from natural causes. Although the twins, Laura and Mae, were kept together in Oakland, their brothers and sisters were sent to live with relatives in Hollister, Modesto, and San Mateo. The oldest brother, Aubrey, went to live on the East Coast. In Modesto, my uncle Finley Bishop used to stomp grapes with Ernest and Julio Gallo when he was young.

I was born in West Oakland, California, the third child of Laura and Turner Wilson. We moved to Berkeley when I was five years old. An older sister Lorraine (now deceased), a younger sister Phyllis, and an older brother Stanley rounded out a closely-knit family.

We were a family of nicknames: my sisters' names were Phee and Weensie, my brother was called Bubba. My nickname was Jebby. Nobody can remember where it came from. When my children found out about "Jebby" it became their favorite way to tease me. When they call me "Mom," they want something—"Jebby" when it's play time.

My Aunt Mae's children Aubrey, Walter, and Ernestine became: Lefty, Heinie and Pigeon. They all lived with my family for a time when Aunt Mae went East. Another cousin, Hazel, became part of the family and lived with us for many years. My mother was the matriarch of the extended family. My mother and father were called "Papa" and "Mama," a habit which continues to this day.

I have five bloods running through my veins and I respect them all. They have served me well. I have been blessed with African and Indian blood, which gave me character and strength. The other three bloods have softened the blows and kept me balanced in a world designed to make me bitter and angry.

As far back as I can remember, I have always worked. I remember pulling my squeaky little red wagon around Berkeley, selling the *Louisiana Weekly* for a nickel. I was only ten years old as I made the rounds of the neighborhood, stopping for a visit here, a snack there. Independent little old lady, Capricorn—that was me. Never a child, I used to sit in the living room talking politics with the elders, while the other children played outside.

I have always felt connected to something bigger than myself. I could neither see it nor hear it, but I could feel it. It was separate from my mother and father, yet it was a feeling of warmth and protection.

As day-to-day problems of growing up began to take over, however, I was subconsciously aware that I could call on an inner presence when needed. This inner awareness grew with me over the years, and one day I would realize the protection it gave me in times of crisis. It never interfered with the life process: I made mistakes, felt pain, went my own way—but it was always there to fall back on.

As a result, I have been blessed with a feeling of comfort: solitude without being lonely, being held in a time of pain, a feeling of being loved unconditionally. So growing up Black, during the Great Depression—I felt rich.

Sunday was my favorite day. Papa got up early and cooked a big breakfast for us before we went to church. Papa was a chef and loved to cook. He always put on a big pot of coffee. I would follow him around the kitchen as he made hot biscuits, fried pork chops with country gravy, cooked grits, eggs, and vegetables. Everybody had Victory gardens in those days (as part of the World War II programs), so Papa would pick fresh greens from the garden.

While we were at church he would start cooking dinner. Usually roast chicken, candied yams, mashed potatoes, vegetables and always coleslaw. Everything was fresh from our garden. Then Papa would put on his coat and walk over to Stubby's Pool Hall on Sacramento Street, where he was a Sunday regular, to shoot pool with the guys. He would often return home with total strangers who would be seated at the dinner table. He also had a few drinks with his friends before they all headed home for a home cooked meal. Mama usually had a fit, and would say, "your father's home again and he's three sheets in the wind," which meant he had too much to drink. She didn't like strangers sitting at her table in front of the children, "carrying on." Papa would take her aside and say "Laura, the men are hungry, they have no place to go." That would usually quiet Mama down, and we would all sit down and enjoy a Sunday dinner. I met some very interesting people at that table: some of them had been family men, others tradesmen or seamen, and some of them had fascinating tales to tell. Through some miracle, like the "loaves and the fishes," there was always enough food for everyone.

On Monday, Papa was back on the grueling job schedule. Looking back, I can see this was Papa's way of enjoying his day off, making new friends, and opening his home to others less fortunate. It was my first lesson in sharing.

My mother often recalled the San Francisco fire and earthquake in 1906. As a little girl, she, along with others, thought it was the end of the world. She went down to the port to watch survivors come across on the ferries, to be warmly received and cared for by the people who lived in Oakland. Most of the injured went to Providence Hospital. When she talked of her young years growing up in Oakland, it reminded me of my own experiences.

We had all the necessary elements of family and community: love, warmth of friendship, and most of all, a happy childhood. We were beneficiaries of parents who treasured having a family because they had both lost their parents so young.

My young years were spent in the flatlands of West Oakland. Our family lived very simply. I can remember catching pollywogs in the estuary, where Jack London Square now stands, and watching red trains running up and down Seventh Street. The Oakland Tribune Building (headquarters of the newspaper by the same name) was the tallest building in Oakland.

During that time, in less affluent communities, economics, not race, decided who your neighbor was, so we grew up next to Portuguese, Italians, Japanese, Chinese, Irish, Polish, Germans and Greeks. I remember meeting Senator Nicholas Petris (of Greek extraction) many years later, when I worked for the California State Legislature. While having dinner one night, I mentioned being born on Seventh and Union Streets, "way down in West Oakland;" Nick bet me he had lived further "down" than I had. He won. Nick had lived at Seventh and Wood streets. That was way down.

I was born inside a little United Nations and didn't know it at the time. It was an introduction to the world at large and that exposure would allow me to move with ease among other races for the rest of my life. If there was a plus for Black children growing up in that kind of neighborhood during that time before racial ghettos set in, it was friendships developed that would last a lifetime.

When the Japanese were interned during World War II, we were one of many families that moved from our home and moved into a Japanese home to take care of it while they were away. We took pictures of their home and garden regularly, to let them know that everything was being maintained as they would have wanted.

My first little friend in Berkeley was Shigero Morita who lived next door. He taught me early on how to count to ten in Japanese.

When we moved to Berkeley around 1930, during the Great Depression, I was five years old. It was a suburb, with only about 2,000 Black people living there at the time. My father soon became a community leader. Back in those days, economic need, not race, was the issue so the people coming to meetings at our house were not only Black, but German, Swedish, Italian, Polish, Irish and Jewish. There were no jobs, and people were unable to pay their rent or buy food. Many of them were recent immigrants who were not yet fluent in the English language. There were no Food Banks back then, no soup lines. There was no organized effort to get food to people, just an inadequate welfare program that could not take care of all those in need. Papa knew the Chief of Police very well, so he called him one day and told him that unless food was brought to the families in the flatlands of Berkeley, the men were going to march on the supermarket at Ashby and Sacramento streets, break the windows and take the food. They did not want to do it, being law-abiding citizens, but they and their families were starving.

I can remember very plainly, one morning when a police car drove up in front of our house on Ashby Avenue, and the policemen dropped off a large carton of groceries on our front porch. The scene was repeated all over Berkeley, and a real food riot was avoided.

Years later, while at KQED, I would interview author Tillie Olsen, author of "Silences," one of the first books about women finding their voices in literature, and I learned that she and her husband, Jack, used to come to those meetings. What a reunion that was! I had first met Tillie Olsen when the producer of our program *"Womantime"* at KQED invited her to be a guest on the show. After an initial reluctance she agreed, and during a break in our interview, I found out she knew my father very well. Tillie and Jack had attended the meetings at our home, and both thought very highly of my father.

Papa was a self-educated man as he had only finished the sixth grade. He read much and loved politics. He loved showing me the difference between intelligence and book learning. "One questions," he used to say, "while the other simply regurgitates." Papa's one concern was to teach me to think for myself, even if I disagreed with him. He taught me to question everything. If I read a newspaper, what was its editorial policy? Who wrote the article? What were the politics of the columnists? If it was a book, who was the author? Why did he write the book? This was all very challenging stuff for a girl of 14.

Mama, on the other hand, hated politics. The only real arguments she and Papa ever had were over his political associations. Mama was always home, she never belonged to organizations, or clubs. She lived only for her children. I can never remember coming home from school when my mother wasn't there.

What a safe harbor that was during those crucial years of growing up! It gave me a sense of security and the feeling that if I ever fell, someone would always be there to catch me, and there always was.

We grew up with parents who taught us we could do whatever we wanted to do, be whatever we wanted to be, provided we were willing to work hard and make sacrifices. We never had a "place"—our "place" was wherever we wanted it to be. That's how my parents raised me and how I raised my children. It would be many years before I would find out that all the wonderful things I saw, read and heard about were never really intended for me.

Mama knew it, Papa knew it, but they never once mentioned it to me. Thank God they didn't tell me, or I might have carried out a self-fulfilling prophecy carefully put together by the dream makers of America, with such catch words as welfare, poverty programs, economic opportunity programs, etc. A whole group of people are being programmed not to perform and give to society, only to take, then they are penalized for taking it.

I clearly remember my counselor at Berkeley High School telling me that even though I had a B average, qualifying me for the University of California, I should not go to college. "You should become a hairdresser or secretary, because," she continued, "there's really nothing for your people in the business world."

I later found out they were telling all the Black students the same thing. This was the kind of counseling Black children received during my era. Our school system helped produce takers, not givers, and the system must bear responsibility for it. I remember in 1975, returning to Berkeley High to talk to a class of young Black students and laughing at what my counselor had advised me in 1941. The students said, "Don't laugh, Mrs. Lange, they are still counseling us that way." A Black counselor then told me she was leaving because she was being reprimanded for motivating Black children in the wrong direction—*up*. I was appalled, remembering all the wonderful class reunions I had attended at this excellent school, particularly the twenty-year class reunion where warm and genuine feelings were expressed between classmates, longing for the good old days. I wondered what they would think of all this.

It was so good to see everybody, and hug my old teachers. I wonder if they ever knew what the counselors were telling us? Did they know they were trying to kill our dreams? What a waste of a natural resource. What if "sputnik" was rambling around in the mind of a little Black child who had been rerouted from mathematics to machine shop?

I found out how important it is to dream. Without a dream you cannot move one inch. If the energy does not go forth, the wheels of life do not spin. The ghetto was where you stifled a dream! I decided that if my children could dream, I would work my fingers to the bone for them to have their dream. No one would deprive them of the chance to become whatever they wanted to become. That is every child's inalienable right, and no teacher, counselor, or parent, has a right to stand in the way of their dreams.

Through nature, Papa taught us to love. Each one of us had a time to grow our garden. He taught us very carefully how to plant a seed, water and care for the plant, shield it, when necessary, from uncertain weather conditions, and then watch the plant become strong and independent. He said the same theory must be applied to human beings. Some are not as strong as others and need more love and care. One day he said he was planting a strawberry plant which was very hard to grow in the Northern California climate. He took a small patch of white sheet, placed it on four little sticks over the plant, which protected it from too much sun or rain, until it was strong enough to stand on its own. We grew a nice little strawberry plant ripe with berries.

Papa could make anything grow. When people had trouble with their plants, he showed them how to make them grow. He taught us that we could heal ourselves with food. He said there is a food for every illness. We never had a doctor; we didn't need one. There was never sickness in our house.

After a lifetime of good health, both Mama and Papa died in their late eighties. As I watch the current trends toward holistic medicine and the return to health foods, I realize how fortunate we were to have lived a lifetime on wholesome food, free of wonder drugs that haven't been properly tested. Psychosomatic illness was something we understood even back then. You can make yourself sick by what you think.

Papa saw to it that my children had their garden, and many years later, my son Ted would write a screenplay called **Passing Through**, which Larry Clark, a UCLA graduate student, made into a film for his thesis. Their film received the Locarno Film Festival Award in Switzerland in 1977. Ted asked me to go see it at the Pacific Film Archives in Berkeley. The film starred Clarence Muse, and when I heard Muse saying my father's words about nature and reverence for the land, I realized Ted had remembered everything his grandfather had taught him. When I asked him why he didn't tell me what the film was about, he said, "I wanted to see if you remembered."

Papa said the earth was like a woman, and planting a seed in the earth was just like the male planting his seed in the womb of a woman. There was a time to plant, a time to grow, a time to harvest and then a time to rest. If you worked her too hard, she would not give forth a good harvest. Most of all he implanted in our minds the concept that the earth was a living thing and was to be treated as such. We were a part of everything around us, and we must always live harmoniously with nature. We must treat our bodies with the same care. If you took good care of your body, it would take good care of you. It all sounded so simple that I could never understand why *so* many people did just the opposite.

Mama, on the other hand, was a strong, tough, resilient woman who fought like a wildcat for her children. Nothing much got past her and she held the family together. Mama dressed very simply, and wore her hair straight back in a bun. She rarely went to the hairdresser, and wore no makeup. She was very fair, with hazel colored eyes; it pained her no end when she was asked to explain who those "little brown children" belonged to. I remember whenever Mama came to the classroom, the teacher would ask me to point out my mother. I'd point to Mama standing in a group of White mothers and the teacher would always say: "I don't see your mother, Geraldine." Her face would turn red when Mama came up and introduced herself.

Mama had been raised in the Baptist Church. Back in the early 1920s, the only major Black church was Third Baptist Church in San Francisco. Its pastor was the Rev. James Hugh Kelley, and Mama and her twin, Aunt Mae, would cross the bay from Oakland every Sunday to attend. After Mama married and had her family, she began to stay home on Sundays. Papa did not go to church, but they saw to it that we did. We belonged to Mt. Pleasant Baptist Church (now McGee Avenue Baptist Church).

One Easter Sunday, however, Mama decided she wanted to be baptized. She had been christened as a child, but had always wanted to go under the water. That Sunday Sunrise service, we all got baptized: Mama, Lorraine, Phyllis, Stan, and I went under the water. Papa stayed home and fixed breakfast. His church was the whole world.

Every morning of their forty-eight years of married life, Papa brought Mama's coffee to bed before he went off to work. Papa was a chef, so Mama rarely cooked. I can vividly remember my parents' loving acts of kindness toward each other. They found contentment in doing things for the children; they read to us and told us stories.

Some of the stories were tough to hear. Papa hid much of the bitter part of his southern childhood from us until much later in our lives, when he felt we were old enough to hear about the treatment of Blacks in the South. He had spent his childhood in Anniston, Alabama and the stories were not pretty. He withheld them as long as he could so we would not grow up bitter. It was a wise decision.

As a child he had witnessed lynchings. He saw an entire family lynched. The woman, who was about eight months pregnant, was hanging from a limb of a tree, when Papa suddenly saw her baby hanging out of her. He also saw Black women, almost nine months pregnant, beaten for not working hard enough. Since they could not lie flat because of the size of their stomachs, Papa saw the men dig holes in the ground so that they rested their protruding bellies in the hole, while being beaten.

He could barely tell us the stories, but he knew we had to know if we were to live in the real world. It was so painful for him to tell us about the cruelty in the world, the inhumane things people did to each other for no reason other than race hatred. Those stories would affect me in many ways. I had the benefit of a close-knit and loving family. Because of that I didn't hate anyone. Papa taught us to always fight for what we believe in, but not to hate our enemy, because that would ruin our lives with bitterness, sickness and pain. The emotional baggage was not worth it.

This is the history Black children grew up with, history no one wanted to tell—hidden history that shaped our lives. America is still paying the price.

Papa always taught us to speak up. If someone is trampling on your self-esteem, let them know it. We were taught never to value your job more than your beliefs. Even though I was ususally one of the pioneer Black women in most of my jobs, I didn't mind putting my self worth over the prestige of the position.

This country is so tied up in guilt and denial that when a person speaks up when they see something wrong, it makes people nervous. You are supposed to keep quiet or you will be punished. That was the price we had to pay in slavery, and it rendered many of our people impotent. I believe if you truly want to be free you must pay a price. Much of this country is blind to its own racism, so when you keep quiet you make it easier to deny that racism exists. You hurt not only yourself but those perpetrating the crime. That is why America still pays the price for slavery and cannot bring itself to apologize. This country feels it has done nothing wrong, and each denial buries it deeper into the subconscious of this country. That is not a prescription for healing.

Speaking up does not mean you hate anyone. It means you value yourself and hold people accountable for their actions. Until we do that—as a nation—none of us will be free. These were the principles of accountability that my father instilled in all of his children.

My brother, Stan Wilson, embodied my father's principle of standing up for one's beliefs. During the era of McCarthyism, my brother was blacklisted and removed from his job as a postman because he sang at the home of Vincent Hallinan, a controversial figure during the fifties who was very active in civil rights. To support his family, Stan had to make a full-time job out of folk singing. When he rose to become a major star, we had to convince Mama that it was all right for him to be a performer. She didn't like it that Stan was appearing in nightclubs, because she thought everybody in show business "took dope." We finally coaxed her to go the Hungry I, where she reluctantly stood up when Stan introduced his "Mom."

Jerri

I remember being forbidden to set foot in a nightclub until I graduated from high school. When I was finally allowed, it was on Graduation Night. It was unthinkable that I would be allowed to nightclub in San Francisco without being properly chaperoned, so I was accompanied by the whole family.

The older I get the more I realize what the family means to each one of us. For instance, I can remember when we all gathered together for a night on the town, back in 1952, first to see an exhibit of my cousin Heinie's art at the Iron Pot restaurant, eating a great Italian dinner, and winding up at the Hungry I to listen to my brother Stan, sing folk songs. It was a high point for me because so many of the clan had gathered together. I remember wishing that that night would last forever.

Stan had helped Enrico Banducci launch the Hungry I, and had written songs for the Kingston Trio. I remember the night Stan said Enrico was trying out a new act. It was a guy by the name of Mort Sahl, who went on to become an icon of political of satire in the in the 60's and 70's, during the years of the Vietnam War and the Johnson and Nixon administrations. I had seen him backstage, waiting to go on. Nervous as a cat, he had a newspaper rolled up in his hand. It became his trademark.

Thinking back, it is a wonder that we went into show business at all. Even when I started appearing on television, Mama never got caught up in it. I remember having to remind her when my show was on. She never bragged about me being on television. If that's what I wanted to do, then it was all right with her, but she did not have to fully participate in the whole thing. I have a feeling, however, were she alive today, she would have been glued to the television set every time her grandson, Ted, sailed across the screen on the *Love Boat* series. She adored her grandchildren.

The strength and love I received from that solid base of family would carry me through many pitfalls and repeated attempts to make me feel less than I was.

I had been taught to give things up, shed skins along the way, but never, never, never, let anyone touch the essence of who I really am. As long as I preserve that, I may walk around in rags, but still carry the richness of soul. And everyone who looks on my face will know I still have it. One has to hang onto it. It's worth its weight in gold. There is talk of returning to the extended family. I could not have made it without my family. No bank ever says to you, "Pay it back when you can." No hospital or rest home gives the loving care and concern to the elderly that they receive from their family.

One of my first mentors was Assemblyman W. Byron Rumford. I had known Byron since I was a child. Rumford's Pharmacy was the only Black-owned drug store in our neighborhood. We all called Byron "Doc." He and his wife Elsie encouraged young people to get an education and genuinely took an interest in us. He gave me my first introduction to politics, which I had taken an interest in from conversations with my father. Rumford, along with D.G. Gibson, the first black political activist in Berkeley, instilled political awareness in many youngsters back in the early '40s. D.G. formed a strong group of community leaders who helped to elect Byron Rumford to the California State Assembly where he became the first Black Assemblyman elected from Northern California. In 1952, I went to work for him as he struggled to pass Fair Employment Practices and Fair Housing laws for several years. Both laws were finally enacted into State law.

In later years, Rumford would run for the Senate, lose, and wind up working with Cap Weinberger in the Office of Budget and Management in Washington, D.C. He was honored by the State Legislature when they named the W. Byron Rumford Freeway (on Highway 24) in his honor, a much deserved accolade to a man who labored long and hard in the vineyards.

Much has been written about Blacks in America, particularly about the racism, poverty and hopelessness of the ghetto. What has not been written, except on rare occasions, is the joy and love and pure fun of growing up as Black children in warm, loving communities. We often hear people of all races say, "I never knew we were poor, because we had such a rich, loving family atmosphere."

In the Bay Area, though there were signs of covert racism, we never paid attention to it. We had a community that was close-knit. Everyone knew each other; our families took care of the entire neighborhood. We had dansants, dancing at San Pablo Park, and sporting events and cultural gatherings at De Fremery Park. In social clubs like the "Teenagers of the '30s and '40s," grandparents, parents and grandchildren got together for annual events. "The Californians," organized twenty-four years ago, in 1978, is a charitable organization which serves senior citizens in the Bay Area. The members are people, including myself, who grew up in Oakland and Berkeley, went to grade school together, and have remained friends since childhood.

Another ongoing gathering is the tradition of family reunions. Every year, our family, organized by Steve Striplin, comes together with all the siblings, to trade stories and exchange greetings. Dr. Barbara Cannon, a longtime friend and educator, interviews each member of the family. Another friend of mine, Mickey Mayzes, a television director and videographer, televises the whole occasion. We now have videotapes of our gatherings for our family archives, to hand down to those who come after us.

Former Mayor Lionel Wilson played tennis at De Fremery Park as a young man, and continued playing throughout his life. He also played baseball at San Pablo Park. Such great athletes as Curt Flood, Bill Russell, Joe Morgan, Vada Pinson, Frank Robinson and Joe Gaines were developed at De Fremery Park. It was Jazz musician Joel Dorham (brother of legendary jazz musician and songwriter Kenny Dorham), who first told me about the great athletes who came out of Oakland, all born within a small radius of each other. These men were not only great athletes, they instigated change in their chosen professions. Ron Dellums also came out of this community to distinguish himself as a political activist and an outstanding Member of Congress. It was Ron who trained and nurtured Representative Barbara Lee, who courageously became the only Member of Congress to vote against the war in Iraq. The rich diversity of the Oakland community was also the home of Huey Newton, founder of the Black Panther Party. Internationally known musicians John Handy and M.C. Hammer both grew up in Oakland. Morrie Turner, the first African American cartoonist to be published in major newspapers around the country, was also an Oakland and Berkeley native. We knew each other as children, went to school together and many years later he appeared on my television show. Morrie's comic strip, "Wee Pals," features children of all races and was inspired by his own background of growing up in the diverse neighborhoods of Oakland and Berkeley. We had a wonderful atmosphere of building leadership along with athletic prowess and creativity. I think it is time for the Black community to reflect on the leadership of that day, and ask some very hard questions about where that leadership has gone.

I hope some future writers will record and publish the upside of our lives in America, particularly in California. Only our torment perpetuated by a system of mental and physical abuse has been recorded in the press and deemed worthy of attention. Our joy of growing up in America, while overcoming oppression, has not.

I married young, while still in Berkeley High School. At sixteen, I had started dating a young man, a pre-med student named Donald Reid. He was from an old California family; his grandparents were very active in the Third Baptist Church in San Francisco, where the family lived. So the courtship was encouraged by both families. The following year, Don proposed and we had a large church wedding at St. Columba's Catholic Church in Oakland. Donald's mother had raised her two children as Catholics, so, I agreed to take instruction in the Church. It was barely a year when Don and I both, realized that we were too young for marriage. We parted amicably and remained friends. We divorced, and I went back to McGee Avenue Baptist Church.

I was twenty-one years old before I would marry again. The Veterans Administration was hiring lots of new people to work on insurance plans and the pay was very good. The building was located in downtown Oakland, and our particular office took up the entire floor. I had heard about an extraordinarily good-looking guy, named Ted Lange, who was cutting a wide swath through the ladies. I decided to head the other way.

One day, after trying to catch my eye on numerous occasions, he cornered me and asked to take me out. I refused. How on earth could I ever handle a guy like that? He persisted, so I told him I would only go out with him with another of his friends to chaperone. I ended up with not one, but two handsome men as escorts and I began to relax as

I found out more about him. Ted turned out to be very much like my father; he was his own person.

In a highly publicized event during the 1940s, Ted was one of the seven Black Seabees who had sued the Navy Department and Secretary Knox for denying them the opportunity to take the test to become Naval Officers. He was also a gifted actor, deep into Little Theatre productions, and wanted to pursue that as a career. He had performed in Nick Stewart's Ebony Showcase in Los Angeles.

He had a deep bass voice, like Paul Robeson, and had been a star on his debating team at Tuskegee Institute, winning many debates against Eastern colleges.

One night, Ted showed up alone for one of our dates, and we were a twosome after that. Somewhere along the way he told me I was the woman he wanted to be the mother of his children, and we were married four months later, after a whirlwind courtship.

The marriage had some wonderful moments, but when the children arrived, Ted returned to his former lifestyle, going out drinking with the boys. I began to feel lonely and neglected.

To make matters worse, Ted lost his job at the VA. He began drinking more and more. When a man thinks for himself, questions what he reads, and arrives at conclusions on his own, he threatens many, no matter what color he is. If he happens to be Black, he is in double trouble. The system simply does not respond positively to people it cannot control. Ted was exceptionally intelligent and never hesitated to express unpopular opinions about racism in the U.S. He used to visit churches and recite a poem entitled *"Black Boat."* The poem was the story of the Black sailors killed in the Port Chicago blast.

Every job Ted applied for, he was told he was overqualified. When he finally decided to become a California State Highway Patrolman, as a last resort, he passed the examination, but failed the orals (a former college champion debater). He went to Los Angeles to pursue an acting career, leaving me and the children behind.

I don't believe either of us was ready for marriage. The children came too quickly, and, the added responsibility of going back to work so soon after the children were born added strain on an already shaky relationship. I wanted to stay home with the children, as my mother had done, and I deeply resented leaving them to go back to work. Now, society is beginning to realize that we have sacrificed our children and stability of the family by taking the woman out of the home.

When a marriage ends, there is such a feeling of frustration, anxiety and loneliness that you can't express. I was too hurt to cry. Even with my family around me, I felt rejected and alone. There is also a sense of failure, because no matter who is to blame, you know that you contributed to that failure.

I did not realize at the time that many years later I would be fighting the same forces Ted had fought when I entered the television business.

Over the years, Ted and I remained good friends. He became a successful businessman in Los Angeles, remarried a wonderful woman and had two more children.

CHAPTER II

MOTHERHOOD

Facing the world alone, to raise children after a divorce is a difficult thing to accept. You look at the long years ahead and wonder if you are up to it. There is not a light at the end of the tunnel that you can see.

My good fortune was having a close-knit family who soon rallied around me. Although I had the responsibility of working and taking charge of my children, my family was there every step of the way. My children had many relatives and loving grandparents as part of our extended family. Even then, it was difficult to make the transition, and I have great admiration for those young women who take on that responsibility all by themselves.

My first thought was to maintain my job status and pay off outstanding bills. A long term goal was to return to school. I had good grades in high school and wanted to go to college. Several years would pass before I could make it happen. The good feeling came from having a plan.

By 1959, seventeen years had passed since I graduated from Berkeley High School. My children were still young: Ted was eleven, Mike was ten, and James eight years old. I took the entrance exam at Merritt College and scored 98.2 in the English section, prompting my counselor to declare me a future writer. She changed my major to English Literature and told me I would thank her later. She was right.

It changed my life. English Literature introduced me to all the great writers and I began to look at the world through different eyes. I was lucky to get assigned to English 1A with Professor Douglas Baugh. He was a remarkable teacher who drew the best from his students. When he saw I had to rush home from work in San Francisco, cook for three children and then make it to class, he told me I could come at 7:30 p.m. instead of 7:00 p.m., as long as I turned in my assignments. That accommodation meant a great deal and also gave me the feeling I had a teacher who believed in me. I got an A in that class and was on my way. Instead of dwelling on the difficult situation I was in, I began to open and expand my mind to new ideas. The world became a bigger place. Somehow as I grew intellectually, my problems became smaller. I began to take control of my life and realized I could do it alone. What a feeling of relief that was. I grew up fast. I engaged the children in almost everything, and we became closer. Facing adversity together is the best way to build a foundation. By the time I finished one year of college, I was on my way to better jobs, and finally the beginning of what would be a new career. The breaks I got in the newspaper and television business can be traced directly back to my decision to go back to college. After the divorce, I had reached a turning point in my life and had made the right choice.

In 1964 my father died. He had lived a long, healthy life. After retiring, he worked as a gardener around pesticides, and he became ill. We did not know what we know now about DDT and other pesticides. He loved taking care of nature, but did not know the hazards. After a brief illness, my father died, and received a military burial at Golden Gate National Cemetery in Colma. It was a very impressive funeral, as they played "Taps" and fired guns. The military officers handed my mother a folded American flag.

After the funeral, Mama quietly announced that she could not go back to the house because "Papa isn't there." So we packed up her things and moved her to my bedroom at our house. I slept on a couch in the foyer for the next three years. Bringing Mama to my house turned out to be a blessing. She looked after the children while I was at work.

Jerri

In 1976, while I was in Paris, my mother died. I remember it vividly because I felt strange that day and tried to get a plane back to the States, but could not get a reservation. The airline ticket clerk told me, "Every American on European soil is on their way back to America for the Bicentennial celebrations!" I called my sister Phyllis on my return home, and her voice broke: "Mama's gone," she said. I went numb. I could hardly believe it. "I tried to reach you in Stockholm, but you had just left the day before. Michael got hold of Ted and Jimmy, so there wasn't anything more you could have done." I thought of my feelings in Paris that day, and decided that was probably the very day and hour that my Mother had died.

"Mama's gone." Two little words. What a lifetime of memories I conjured up in that moment. Mama, whose lap I had curled up in whenever I felt the need to be petted. Mama, whose warm, lovely hands had only to touch my forehead when I was sick, and make me well. Mama, who never kept an immaculate house, so whenever other kids could not "mess up" their own houses, they came over and "messed up" ours. All the parties and gatherings were held at our house because the kids could stomp as loud as they wanted to and never get thrown out, and in the middle of the living room floor, up would jump Papa, forefinger up, doing his "Indian Dance." After that, he would recite the "Preacher and the Bear." I remembered Papa's opening line to any guy that hit our front door: "How about a game of Pinochle?"

Papa had gone, and now Mama. How I missed them. How it hurt inside. First one shoe, now the other had dropped, and I would go barefoot for the rest of my life.

Fate was kind to me and my children. Many women have asked me how I managed to have a career and raise three sons in a working class community—and survive. It takes hard work and a lot of love.

I found out early—children do not listen to what you say—they watch what you do. So I found I had to back up what I said with action. I made rules and kept them. Contrary to what they say, children want and need discipline. I drew the line on what kind of behavior I would allow in the home. Children will take advantage of indecision and weakness of parents. I always knew where my children were and they always knew where I was. With these admonitions in place, one can give children plenty of love. Discipline without love leads to children who grow up harsh and mean-spirited. My motto: cuddle but do not coddle.

I remember spanking my children but also kissing wherever that switch hit! That simple act meant I disapproved of what they were doing, but I still loved them. That's the balance that is key to everything else.

I gave my children chores to do at home. It is excellent training for future work habits. As the children grew up and wanted extra money, they had to earn it: paper routes, washing and polishing cars, cutting lawns. Ted even took an after school job as a janitor at Oakland Technical High School, while attending there. He later became Student Body President. At age 16, Mike became a caregiver, moving in with a family in Piedmont, to take care of their father, a retired wealthy businessman, who had suffered a stroke. My youngest son, James, had a sandwich business when barely out of his teens. He bought all of the products and hand-made the sandwiches himself. One of his main clients was Kaiser Industries, where he had previously worked as a mail clerk.

I reminded my children of how my father expressed his love to my mother by bringing her coffee to bed with a kiss on the forehead— every morning of their 48 years together. If they wanted to be a King, I informed them, they would have to have a Queen, and they could begin with me. When Ted and Mike were barely 6 and 7 years old, I would make the coffee, and they would take turns bringing it to bed, with a kiss on my forehead every morning. To learn about love you have to do loving things. You could hear the grumbling all the way to the kitchen. Then one morning I overheard them arguing over whose turn it was to "bring Mommy's coffee to bed." I suggested they team up: one of them could bring the saucer and the other the cup; the two items came together at the appropriate time. From then on it became a ritual. As they grew older, they learned to make the coffee, and coffee in bed became not only one of my most pleasant moments in the morning, it was also a lesson in love for the children.

Most children act out the lessons you are trying to teach them. Our family held meetings which led to forming a family corporation. When the children were still young, they each had an equal vote on how our home was run. We respected each other. Respect begins in the home.

Years later, we would form a family corporation—when Ted was in Hollywood. It was easy. We had done it already.

When I worked at the *San Francisco Chronicle*, drama critic Paine Knickerbocker gave me tickets to the Peking Opera, on its very first visit to San Francisco. I remember going back home to Oakland, cooking dinner, and hauling the children on a bus back to Chinatown for the performance. They absolutely loved it. They were only teenagers, but can still recall everything that took place that evening, especially because most of the performers were barely teenagers themselves. They even remember some of the dance steps. When the lights came up during intermission I remember everyone staring at us. Most of the audience was Chinese, and we were the only Black people. Knickerbocker also gave me tickets to almost every stage performance at the Geary and Curran Theatres. So the children were exposed to live theatre at a very young age.

While they read the usual children's classics, I made sure they also read Shakespeare and studied *King Lear, MacBeth, and Hamlet,* to learn how the "palace intrigue" they read about was alive and well in the ghetto. The boys also learned to play chess at a young age. At first they played with the simple figures that come with the game. As they grew older, I introduced them to the human figures as "real" players in the game of life. They could be anyone on the chess board, except the "pawn". That was the one who was sacrificed first. A great deal can be learned through the playing of games; that is why the military initiated "war games", to teach soldiers how to react in times of war.

We had a chance to buy a set of the Great Books, and we met with the salesman and decided together. I told them the books contained information they would need to do research on their papers throughout high school and college. I agreed to make the down payment, and they were to keep up the monthly payments. The books belonged to them, because they had paid for them. Years later, after Michael had graduated from UC Berkeley, he packed the bookcase and the Great Books in his car, and delivered them to Ted, who was now raising his sons down in Los Angeles. These books have served the family well, taught the children how to read the classics, and to treasure the books because they had to pay for them with hard earned money. My grandsons can now use them and pass them on to their children.

I taught my children to protect themselves with strangers and friends. I warned, "Don't talk to strangers and don't always follow your friends—they may be leading you into trouble." In a working class community, that becomes an overriding issue. In addition, I warned my children about how difficult it is to become "men" in an oppressive society; how I had been programmed by a system to emasculate them and take their "balls." "Don't let me do it," I said. "I won't know I'm doing it," I continued, "so you have to stop me."

From then on, at least once a week, I could count on hearing: "Mother, you're emasculating me again." As I look back, that exercise not only saved their manhood, it saved my womanhood as well!

I never let my children wear me out. When I got tired of coming home to quarrelling children, I called a meeting. Children will respond if you give them a chance to participate in running the home. I told them we would begin a new rule: After I came home from work, they would have the table set, vegetables peeled. The television could be on but the sound would be off. Fighting was prohibited. I needed a half-hour of "Quiet Time". I would take a warm bath, relax in the tub, and wash away all the negative activities of the day. Otherwise I would be spanking them—not for something they did—but out of frustration and stress of the day. They understood and obliged. One day I finished bathing early and came out to the living room. There was Mike on the floor, Ted on top of him with a strangle hold: "Mike, I'm going to knock the devil out of you, as soon as Mommy's Quiet Time is over." It works!

These are true stories that helped a single mother and her children make it through some very tough times. It takes a strategic plan, time, patience and a lot of love to pull it off. After all, this is war.

J e r r i

My children worked because they saw me work—often holding down three jobs—to support the family. I raised my children to "live" not "die" in the ghetto. As they reached their teens, there were greater temptations to get into trouble. But with a lot of care and love, even if they got into trouble, they could get out of it and lead productive lives.

An update on my children:

Ted, my oldest, an actor who is best known for his portrayal of Isaac on the *Love Boat* series, had good luck from the very beginning. He landed a role in *Hair* on Broadway at 22 years old. He went on to win a scholarship at the American Film Institute and became the first recipient of the James Cagney Directing Fellowship Award. After short stints in "That's My Mama", and "Mr. T. and Tina", he hit the jackpot with *The Love Boat*, which sailed the high seas for nine years. He went on to become a first rate writer/director in Hollywood. He directed and starred in *Othello* and is currently finishing *Prophet Nat*, the story of Nat Turner, leader of the slave rebellion in Virginia. Both were filmed by his own production company. He hopes to release *Prophet Nat* this year.

Michael graduated from the University of California at Berkeley with a degree in Political Science, worked for years with at-risk children and was an official with the Oakland Parks and Recreation Department, where he supervised Feather River Camp, located high in the Sierras of California. Michael is also an actor/producer. He has performed *Malcolm X* many times as a one man show and also acted in the play *The Meeting,* a play that portrays the fictional meeting between Malcolm X and Dr. Martin Luther King, Jr. He is working with Ted on *Prophet Nat*. He is currently Operations Manager for the Alice Arts Center in Oakland.

Jimmy, my youngest, is a printer, specializing in uniquely designed business cards. Very independent, he is always there when needed. He exhibits much of his grandfather's "shaman" gifts. He nurtures those in the family who need healing. He has a sharp, quick mind and an ability to see the large picture. He reads encyclopedias the way most people read books. He does not read newspapers or watch television, except occasionally. I'm sure this is from hearing my critiques on how the media impacts our behavior. We have long hours of conversation on social and political subjects, which remind me of the long conversations I used to have with my father.

Both Ted IV and Turner, my grandchildren, are very fine artists. Ted IV has graduated from Pratt Institute of Design in New York, and Turner attends a similar college in New York City. With three wonderful sons and two darling grandsons—I feel blessed.

CHAPTER III

CROSSING THE BAY—
San Francisco Chronicle/City Hall

THE SAN FRANCISCO CHRONICLE

In 1963, Dr. Nathaniel Burbridge, President of the NAACP, along with its members, picketed the *San Francisco Chronicle* to demand that more Blacks be hired for the editorial section of the paper. They were particularly concerned that the editorial department did not reflect the diversity of the community. Frank Collier, who had served as a Black officer in the United States Army, was on the Reuters desk, and a few others were employed in other departments; but the specific request was for a Black woman to be hired in the editorial department. Managing Editor Gordon Pates looked for four months before he hired me. I had been working at the Jewish Community Relations Council in San Francisco for about a year. They urged me to apply for the position of editorial secretary, and I was hired after the first interview.

My three years at the *San Francisco Chronicle* would prove to be the most growing, learning, productive years in my life. I was hired to work for three columnists: Art Hoppe, Charles McCabe (The Fearless Spectator) and Count Marco. In addition, I was secretary to the Executive Editor, Scott Newhall.

My duties were to take dictation for three columnists and the Executive Editor. Although the letters for the columnists were mostly routine, working for the Executive Editor of a major newspaper is quite varied. Routing calls, handling very sensitive information, often becomes intense during threats of strikes or other crisis between management and the workforce. I was sworn to secrecy, while having to mingle with reporters, and it often placed me in an uncomfortable position. I always kept confidential information to myself. I found out how destructive leaks can be when they occur. Such leaks never happened under my watch. It was this trust coming from the front office, that made it easier for me to begin to write articles and an occasional book review for the paper. I had always hoped to become a first-rate journalist on a major newspaper.

"Scotty", as he was affectionately known, was a rebel, an iconoclast, and true to the word: a "breaker of images, destroyer or exposer of shams or superstitions, one who makes attacks on cherished beliefs." He turned out to be another one of the important persons in my life who would help me see what was real and what was not. He did this, not so much through verbal conversation, but by letting me observe how a newspaper is run—from the top. He ran *The Chronicle* with a stern hand. When a memo hit the city room floor with the initials "SN" on it, things moved, immediately.

Scott was a fourth-generation Californian whose family owned most of the farming land in a town called Newhall (near Los Angeles); I was a third-generation Californian, so we shared many stories about the 'good old days'. He loved Jazz and was a great fan of Earl 'Fatha' Hines and Art Tatum. He even presented Hines with the gift of a piano. His main hobby was collecting antique cars which he entered into the 'Concours de Elegance'. We hit it off right away. Everybody told me to watch out for words like "memorabilia" and "bacchanalian" which rolled easily off his tongue during dictation. I solved that problem by simply asking him how to spell them. He always obliged. He usually greeted me with: "How is the Queen of the East Bay this morning?" When my father died, Scott had his name placed in the San Francisco Maritime Museum, because of his military service as a Buffalo Soldier.

Scott had met his wife, Ruth, when she was his journalism teacher at the University of California. Tragedy hit soon when, as a young man on a sailing trip, he gashed his leg, and it had to be amputated. His attitude toward that bit of fate can best be seen in the huge painting of a peg-legged pirate, which hung in his office, along with small cannons, world maps, huge chests, and other memorabilia. The painting closely resembles Scott Newhall. It was at **The Chronicle** that I discovered how closely tied the political world was to a major newspaper. Politicians courted editorial support, which could sway an election one way or the other. And they all made their way through the huge editorial offices, at one time or another. A newspaper is plugged into everything that happens in a city through its reporters. Much that never hits print can be stored away for background information whenever a particular story hits the news. For this reason, reporters, as a whole, are not very impressed by most things or people. They know too much; they are privy to things they cannot print. As far as they are concerned, everybody has clay feet. If they like you, however, they are your friend for life. (In later years, when the television doors would slam tight—I could walk through the city room floor, and chat with old friends).

There were only three Black people on the third floor when I arrived: a library clerk and a copy boy. The third person was the only one in the editorial department—Frank Collier, who was the news correspondent on the Reuters Desk. He was a retired Colonel in the Army. Frank went back to Stanford for his Master's Degree in Journalism. He was promoted to Assistant Wire News Editor in 1955. Later, around 1964, Gloria Davis was hired as a Library Clerk. Gloria had two sons and we talked often about the problem of being a single mother. We became close friends. She was extraordinary. Her dream was to become a teacher of Black children, preparing them to compete in a competitive world. She later became one of the most dedicated Black teachers I have ever known, and I am sure she turned out many Black scholars. The San Francisco Unified School District had the good sense to name the Gloria R. Davis Middle School in her honor.

There is one man who has outlasted almost everyone I met at the paper—Bill German. He is one of the longest running men on the scene. He was City Editor when I arrived, then, over the years after my departure, he became Executive Editor, after Scott Newhall left. He was responsible for my becoming an international correspondent for *The Chronicle*, when he published my article on Africa, during a four-country tour of that country back in 1978: "Black Africa: Facing Up To Its Growing Pains."

Bill looked just like his name: A German with a crew-cut, square jaw, and a no nonsense guy. He was a natural when he headed up the *Newspaper of the Air* at KQED, during its run when *The Chronicle* was on strike. That program became the model for news programs all over the country. Bill was the heart and soul of the show. He recently retired as Executive Editor, and occasionally writes a column for *The Chronicle*.

One of the reporters who became a good friend of mine was Bill Chapin. He was Chief Copy Editor, and he taught me how the stories were put together: the local reporter reports to the city editor who sends it on to the news editor who determines where it will run in the newspaper. (Bill German was news editor at that time.) He orders the trim and headline. It then goes to a copy editor on the Rim (as it is called), who approves it and sends it back to the Chief Copy Editor for final approval. It is then sent to the composing room where the story is ready to go. It is important to know how many people decide what goes into every story that finally makes its way into the newspaper.

The battle for circulation dominance in the San Francisco Bay Area was between the *San Francisco Chronicle* and *The Examiner*. The key to this escalating war was Herb Caen. *The Examiner* lured him away briefly, and their circulation shot up. Herb later returned to *The Chronicle* to much applause and relief.

Herb Caen was the King. He was a primary reason for the large increase in circulation enjoyed by *The Chronicle*. Since his death, no other columnist has taken his place. I am sure whoever tries will find out how difficult it must be to make writing such a column look easy. He had grace and style. When I was being considered as book reviewer for Jack Vietor's *San Francisco Magazine,* Herb called and simply said: "Give the lady the job . . . she can write." I needed no other recommendation.

Jerri

One of the other columnists I was assigned to, as a part-time secretary, was Charles McCabe, a tall, elegant man with British airs. He did not want a secretary at all, and had fired a slew of them in just two years prior. He shared an office with Hoppe. He came in each morning early, knocked out several columns and stalked out of the city room with a bounce; cocky, smiling broadly as he waved ta-ta to those reporters still struggling with a word here, a paragraph there. Hoppe, who sweated blood over each column, used to say, "Jerri, I don't know how he does it." I simply had to come up with a way to stay on the job. Knowing he hated answering letters and did not want a secretary in his hair, one day I marched into his office and said, "Mr. McCabe, I understand you don't want a secretary and I don't want to be one. So why don't we figure out an easy way to do your letters. Why don't you separate the letters you really want to answer and put the rest of them in the top drawer. I'm a good writer, so I will pick them up, answer them and leave them on your desk for signature. That way we don't even have to see each other." He looked up at me perplexed, then smiled. "It's a deal." From then on, whenever I saw McCabe, he gave me a big smile!

Being an editorial secretary to talented men was like being on a roller coaster ride! I had to blend with all their temperaments. Count Marco was an Italian hairdresser, named Marc Spinelli, who had been invented and elevated to royalty by Scott Newhall. As 'Count' Marco, he gave advice to the women of San Francisco and its environs. He was almost a caricature of himself. He had fun with the role he was playing and the women either loved him or hated him. He used to tell me he loved it when they hated him because circulation went up! So he wrote his columns to provoke, and succeeded. I was told Marc would stamp his foot and throw a tantrum; but I liked Marc, so by the time he threw his famous tantrum with me, I was ready for it. I described all this to a friend of mine who was very astute. He told me how to handle it when it came my turn. So by the time Marc had his "tantrum" with me, I waited until he got to the screaming part and simply said: "Marc, stop having intercourse with me." Startled, he just looked at me and said nothing. He never tried it again, and we soon became friends.

The heart and soul of a newpaper rests on the City Room floor. It is where all the action takes place-alive with information, power and excitement. Once I got over my fright, I loved entering its portals, bustling with reporters scrambling to make deadlines. Some could be seen pounding their typewriters, or doing nothing-searching for just the right word to make their story come alive. It was pure energy in action. It is where Abe Melinkoff, City Desk Editor, held court.

Abe, with his black-rimmed monocle covering his eye, was a sight to behold. He would try hard not to laugh, then let the monocle fall, dangling from a long black string, ending with a bow and a beautiful smile, always to applause. He usually embellished his act with a German accent. I learned a great deal from Abe about the practices of the newspaper business; he was always available to answer any questions I might have: choice of stories, which ones made it to press, which ones didn't and why. What was the focus of the story? When to name names and when not to; why the paper always used the word "alleged" to avoid lawsuits, and how television usually picked stories from the morning edition to use on their evening broadcast. This practice remains today.

I published my first article at *The Chronicle* because Count Marco had read a paper I had written for a sociology course at San Francisco State. He helped me re-write it from a research paper into an article, then introduced me to Dick Demorest, the editor of "This World", a section of the Sunday paper. My first article, "The Coming Revolution in the American Negro Family," appeared there. I had never written an article for publication and didn't know where to turn for help. I found it in one of the most unexpected places.

Carolyn Anspacher was the only woman reporter at *The Chronicle* at that time. She came from a very old and respected San Francisco family. She looked very stern and formidable, and did not suffer fools gladly, so I decided to stay out of her way. One day, while I was making my rounds on the third floor, Carolyn came up to me and said, "I hear you're having trouble with your story for the Sunday paper." I almost froze, but recovered enough to answer, "I just can't seem to find the hook." "Well, I'd like to help if I can," she replied. "First, make sure you have a strong opening paragraph. You must grab the reader right away." Carolyn not only helped me get a handle on the story, but helped me write a blockbuster opening paragraph. The story stated that the revolution in the Black community could not happen until the revolution in the Black family took place. The opening paragraph made the observation that the Black Woman would have to relinquish her throne as Queen and share it with the Black Man if he was to become King in his own home. The article was controversial but well received. I also came to know Carolyn much better. She had a great sense of humor, but didn't smile often. When she did smile, her whole face lit up. I found her to be forthright, honest, and dependable. I felt much safer in that atmosphere with her on my side. I am sure her stern demeanor was prompted by the fact that she was the only woman on a floor dominated by men.

I also wrote book reviews for Bill Hogan, the book editor, which led to my reviewing books for *San Francisco Magazine*. I had been moonlighting for *San Francisco Magazine* for the whopping salary of $60.00 per month, when the publisher, Jack Vietor, took me to lunch. Over cracked crab and champagne—he fired me! A man by the name of Casper Weinberger was to be the new book reviewer. Cap Weinberger was a lawyer who loved to write and would bring in a new audience.

Somehow the cracked crab and champagne took precedence over the job, and I told Jack I was impressed with his class act. Then he countered with: "Look how much prestige you'll get by telling people who replaced you."

I'm sure not even Jack Vietor could know how prophetic his words would turn out to be. Cap Weinberger became the Secretary of Defense.

When I finally met Cap Weinberger, I teased him about taking my $60.00 per month job. As it turned out, we eventually had two things in common: we both hosted national PBS programs from KQED (he hosted 'World Press'), and we would both work for Jack Vietor as book reviewers.

The Chronicle political cartoonist was Bob Bastian, a very shy, handsome and talented man. I had noticed him sitting way across the city room next to the windows, always quiet, contemplating his work

Jerri Lange

for the day. With prematurely gray hair that perfectly framed his handsome face, his round eyes, like dark buttons, set perfectly in his head, often caught you directly in their gaze—a gaze that seemed to look right through you.

One morning the story came over the wire services about the bombing of a church in Alabama, which took the lives of four young Black children. They were blown to bits. The bomb had been planted in the church and timed to go off during Sunday School Class.

As we gathered in the wire services room watching the machines pump out the breaking story, bit by bit, details emerged about how terrible the crime really was. Flashbacks of Papa's horror stories about things he had witnessed in Alabama jolted me. I became outraged, angry and full of anguish. As tears began to fill in my eyes, I left. I ran downstairs to my office. A couple of reporters found their way downstairs to offer apologies. I kept thinking: "Those children could have been mine."

Finally it was time to make my way back upstairs to the third floor for my daily walk across the city room. Walking across that long floor, dense with reporters working on news stories of the day, was always intimidating. I felt self-conscious. A bustling beehive of activity, the city room of a major newspaper is a way to really get to know the City. It is an education you will not get elsewhere. These were men who shaped public opinion, made reputations or broke them, either by omission or commission. You could sense the raw power in the air as you identified the powerful men whose bylines made the daily news. Television may flex its muscle and change the course of events from time to time—but nothing will ever replace the sifting down of information that can only take place through the printed word.

It was against this background, across this floor, that I had to walk to get to Art Hoppe's office. I managed to cross it without looking at anyone. I was the first Black woman in the editorial section of the paper, and nobody knew it better than me.

But this particular morning was different. For one thing, I was angry. I slowly started up the stairs, dreading every moment, hoping I wouldn't give away my feelings. When I got upstairs something came

60

over me and I suddenly found the courage to look everyone in the eye as I passed them by. I had to know how they felt, what their reactions were as they covered this story.

I saw many things in people's eyes that day, but most of all I saw shame. No one was prepared for the news that grown White men were now blowing up small, innocent Black children in their place of worship. On the way back, I had to stop at the library to pick up some files. I was totally unprepared for what happened next. As I was waiting for the file, I turned around and saw Bob Bastian headed my way, his piercing gaze flashing clear across the city room floor. He made his way over to me, stood for a second or two, just staring, then blurted out: "How can you stand it? How can you stand this world?"

I stood there stunned! I couldn't move. This quiet, sensitive man had come clear across the city room to show me his pain, and it was seemingly as great as mine.

We stood there, in the middle of a bustling city room floor, both shocked by events that had taken place in another city, but which had touched our souls in a deep place. I think he felt ashamed and hurt that human beings could do this to each other. I wondered if I could find it in my heart for forgiveness. For I truly believe that if we do not forgive and move on—we perish. Bob's gesture had given me hope that other White people were just as shocked and outraged as I was. I turned around to pick up my files, and in that short interval, Bob was gone. He had taken my anger with him.

On September 22, 1970, Bob Bastian's body was found on a lonely beach at Fort Cronkhite in Marin County, near his home. He had committed suicide at age 53.

Those of us who knew Bob wept for him that day. He had seemed to have found his niche as political cartoonist for KQED's *Newsroom* after leaving the **San Francisco Chronicle** in 1968. None of us could sense his inner torment. A quiet, sensitive man, who had seen action as a Marine Major during World War II, Bob could still feel, still love, and it was too much for him to bear. He could walk clear across a city room and, out of deep compassion, tell me how much he hated himself and the ugly world that had taken the lives of four little Black children because he could see how much pain I was in.

Years later, when I was writing this book, I would talk to Mel Wax, anchor for *Newsroom* at the time, who recalled the events that took place. "Everyone had noticed how odd it was that Bob did not show up that afternoon to start preparing for the evening show. We called around and couldn't find him. By the time we went on the air, we were really worried," said Wax. About halfway through the program a call came that Bob's body had been found on the beach. Mel waited until the end of the program and made the first announcement of Bob Bastian's death. He and his fellow reporters, George Dusheck, Ed Radenzel and Jim Benet, gave moving eulogies on their fallen colleague.

The Bob Bastian incident had been an incredible turning point in my life, but it would be Art Hoppe, however, that would mark my most surprising experience at *The Chronicle*. The events that occurred would turn everything upside down in my world.

A very shy man who rarely speaks in public, Hoppe wrote satire and did it with a razor sharp wit, style and a large dose of humanity. He agonized and sweat over each word, every line; answered every letter personally and his answers to readers were just as razor sharp as his columns.

The whole thing began very shortly after I arrived at *The Chronicle*. I had been a roving editorial secretary taking dictation and typing letters for four men. Reporters had hinted that Scott Newhall would dictate difficult letters with words I could not pronounce; Charles McCabe didn't want a secretary at all, and Count Marco would eventually throw a tantrum and stamp his foot. As I have already indicated, I was able to defuse these events before they occurred.

Hoppe was another matter. He was affectionately called the 'House Liberal' and was universally loved by all, including me. It all started out fine and everyone predicted that I would have no trouble there. I was about to explode an assumption that many White people have: they "know" how Black people think. Some of us have problems with liberals, and would like a chance to stop being regarded as children, and we need to be given the respect to solve some of our own problems. Hoppe and I were about to embark on an incident that would bring all of this out in the open and in the end inspire one of his best columns.

J e r r i

I couldn't wait to grab a cup of coffee and head for Hoppe's office, looking forward to a wonderful time of taking dictation then discussing topics of the day: politics, civil rights, women's rights and a host of other things. However, I began to notice a feeling of discomfort on some issues. I felt society had not let Black people work out their own destinies; welfare was crippling our communities by encouraging dependency. We always needed help to get anything done. Entrepreneurship was not encouraged. So Hoppe and I frequently had disagreements.

By the 1990's, all these ideas were finally put into motion by a Democratic President—Bill Clinton—and one cannot imagine that back in the 1960's, this was not on the average liberal's agenda. With the onset of the Civil Rights Movement, these were not popular ideas. Hoppe understood much of this and his columns reflected a man who felt deeply about race problems affecting our society. I agreed with so much he had to say, that it made our subsequent disagreements entirely unexpected. We had so many beliefs in common, I don't think either of us saw it coming. It had to do with who is in control of whose freedom. Many white liberals don't understand what courage it took for runaway slaves to strike out on their own, with just faith and an inner compass directed by God. The stereotype has always been the 'scared darkie' who is afraid of his own shadow. Nat Turner (the slave who led the Southampton Rebellion in 1831) was not held up as a role model. Picture men and women in a strange country, who could not read or write, beaten and mistreated on plantations, hounded by armed men and dogs, if they escaped, not knowing where they were headed; unarmed and facing death every inch of the way. These were people who wanted to be free. If our ancestors were able to pull that off, with support when needed, we can go to the next level as well. So although many well-meaning Whites could understand our need to be free—they differed on how that would be accomplished. Hoppe was at the top of the line in understanding all of this. It was the subtle nuances that got in the way, and it would soon come to a head. Our discussions would bring to light how difficult it is for even enlightened people to grasp the complexities of true equality.

One day I heard Hoppe was not happy with my work, and that my job was on the line. I immediately told Marc and he agreed to talk to Hoppe to see what was wrong. It seems I was not giving enough time to answer all of Hoppe's letters. Marc and Scott agreed to let me give Hoppe as much time as he needed, and so I began taking his letters first; they were now my number one priority. Things went well for a while, but then one day we started talking politics again. The subject was 'White liberals'; they did not understand at the time, that dependence kept us from accepting responsibility, thereby keeping us from true freedom. I finally said I thought the problem was that 'liberals' thought they had to love Black people. "You don't even have to like us. We just want you to respect us," I said. "The same criteria should be used on everyone. You are free to dislike anyone who is not a good person. That is true equality."

Hoppe looked up startled. "But what about the guilt? There's so much guilt."

"Hoppe, we just want to be free," I said. "All we want 'White liberals' to do is take their guilt off our backs and let us grow to our highest potential."

I turned around and left the office. When I got downstairs, I wondered what had come over me. Why did I say those things? But I had to say something; I was smothering to death, and didn't know why. Did he understand what was going on?

The answer came in Hoppe's next column. Not only had he understood, he had written a column so that everyone else would understand as well. It was entitled "For Mental Health, Forget the Negro." The column said in part:

> "I used to care deeply about The Negro. There was no greater advocate than I of equal rights for The Negro, fair housing for The Negro, equal employment for The Negro, freedom of the ballot for The Negro. No one decried racial prejudice more than I. Then one day I suddenly realized I had a deep-seated racial prejudice. Worse, the whole Nation is racially prejudiced. Some White people are prejudiced against The Negro. And some of us are prejudiced for The

Negro. And if most Negroes aren't prejudiced against all
White people, I'd be very much surprised . . . . So I honestly
have come to believe there is only one thing we can do for
The Negro: Forget him. "For The Negro, after all, doesn't
exist. We made him up so we'd have a symbol to talk about
and write about and fight about."

Hoppe had understood it all and had written a column that would
withstand time. We have been invented by a nation that has not come
to terms with slavery and continues to find ways of describing who we
are. Hoppe was ahead of his time and remains so to this day. Many
years later while doing my television show on KBHK, I had to dig up
illustrious guest celebrities. I called and asked Art Hoppe, the man
who never appeared on talk shows, to be my guest. In one of his rare
public appearances he appeared on *San Francisco Today*.

*   *   *

After almost three years at **The Chronicle**, I was invited to lunch one
day and offered a job at City Hall—Personal Secretary to Mayor Jack
Shelley—as the first minority member of the Mayor's personal staff; a
prestigious and well-paying job. I accepted. "Now you'll see the action
from the other side, Jerri," Scott Newhall mused.

The **San Francisco Chronicle** was the place where I made lasting
friendships and it became the launching pad from which I sprang to
make my way in the great City.

On my last day, Charles de Young Theriot, the publisher, came in
Scott Newhall's office while I was taking dictation. He only made rare
appearances so I was flattered when he said, "I hear you're leaving us,
Jerri, going over to City Hall. Don't you like us any more?" he asked.
"Oh, yes, Mr. Theriot, but they made me an offer I couldn't refuse," I
replied.

"Well, keep in touch," he said.

"I will," I replied.

In November, 2000, the **San Francisco Examiner** bought out the
San Francisco Chronicle, merging the two papers.

CITY HALL

My brief excursion into City Hall would be enlightening in ways I would not immediately comprehend. For one thing, I was hand picked, interviewed and hired in one swift, secret move. By the time anybody heard about it, the story was already in the *San Francisco Chronicle*. That's the way politics work.

The year and a half I spent at City Hall went very fast, and served as a lesson in how politics permeate every facet of life. As personal secretary to the Mayor, my job was to take dictation, write thank you notes, and other tasks. I am sure others outside City Hall thought I was privy to all the palace intrigue, but that was not the case.

Much of the business of City Hall takes place outside the office, and if you are not privy to those meetings, you don't really know what is going on. I was there to do a job and I did it. Being the first Black appointee to the Mayor's office upset many people who felt my desk was much too close to power. They needn't have worried.

That all changed however, when the City was threatened by a race riot in Hunter's Point. The Mayor was suddenly beset with a crisis. He faced a showdown because of a series of grievances in the Black Community: lack of jobs, housing and the shooting of a Black teenager.

The Mayor called in his staff to get an opinion about his next move. We were all concerned for his safety. He called us in one by one to ask our opinion on what we should do. Most advised him to handle it by negotiation, if possible. I advised him to go out to Hunter's Point. Police Chief Thomas Cahill said that a group of Hunter's Point youths were headed to City Hall for a showdown. I told the Mayor that all these young people wanted was to be heard. Most of the staff was adamant against it, and suggested that if anything happened to the Mayor, I would be held responsible. Much to my surprise, the Mayor decided to take the chance and go to Hunter's Point. To soften the highly charged atmosphere, Shelley was to give a speech.

I clearly remember the day he brought the speech to me to re-type. It had been initially typed on small, square, expensive, white paper, with a distinctive elite type, blue typewriter ribbon. I immediately recognized it as having come from the office of Scott Newhall. I should know, I had typed on that typewriter and used that same unique paper for more than three years. Scotty had written the speech the Mayor was about to deliver so eloquently. The speech was so sensitively written that many people would later tell me they thought I had written it.

I realized I didn't know who anybody was anymore, because everybody was really somebody else. People at certain levels of power were playing dual roles, all designed to hold things together, with little concern about who took the credit. I computed this fact up to its highest level, nationally and internationally, and the possibilities were staggering. It gave me respect and admiration for the many unsung heroes who quietly patch up the world as headlines blaze across the front page—hardly ever telling the real story. I wondered how many such practices take place all over the country, particularly in the South, to prevent bloodshed from occurring in this country.

In the hours preceding the showdown, we all had dinner in the Mayor's office. Chief Cahill joined us to advise us about possible violence. The Mayor's chauffer took off his jacket to have dinner, and I saw for the first time he was carrying a gun in a holster, strapped around his chest. I had known he was a former policeman, but as many times as I had been driven around in the Mayor's limousine, I had never noticed the gun. Everything began to appear surreal. It seemed that I was in the middle of what could become a very violent scene and there was no way out.

After dinner, Chief Cahill and the Mayor, with plenty of police protection, left for Hunter's Point. The women stayed behind.

Jack Shelley was no stranger to violence. In the 1930s, he had participated in one of the bloodiest, violent union strikes on the waterfront in the history of San Francisco. He was a member of the Bakery Wagon Driver's Union, and had been beaten by the police. He had the scars on his forehead to prove it, and loved retelling the story.

The young Black "turks" of Hunter's Point must be given a great deal of credit for giving the Mayor a chance to speak, and thus avoiding a full scale race riot in San Francisco. They all put on black armbands and promised to keep the peace. Mayor Shelley agreed to see them at

City Hall. It was an historic day when these young men came marching into City Hall, some for the first time, assembled in the Mayor's office to bring peace to the City. I would see some of these young men over the years as some of them became part of the City Hall workforce, particularly in the community.

As Mayor Shelley's first term was ending, speculation arose about his running for a second term. He had not been well, and one day Mel Wax came rushing over to ask whether the Mayor was in the hospital and about to announce that he would not seek a second term. He also said it was rumored that Joe Alioto would run instead. All of this was news to me. I had remembered a call coming into the office from Joe Alioto, but that was it. The next day the Mayor held a press conference from the hospital, and said he had decided not to run. The following day, Joseph Alioto announced his intention to run for Mayor. It was another example of the 'real' business of City Hall being carried out elsewhere.

I was reminded of my years at *The Chronicle*, where reporters had connections to everything that was going on in the City, and published only "the news that's fit to print." If something was going down, they usually had information before anyone else. The only question was, whether or not to print it. The power elite decided that—another example of managed news.

I would leave City Hall feeling I had only peripherally participated in the City's history. It would be years later before I understood the backhanded way we are given information, and that learning does not always come the way you expect.

I learned how "privileged" information can be withheld no matter how close you are to it; that there is a "grapevine" that only 'insiders' have access to, and if you are not a member, you don't get the information. That's powerful stuff you won't find in any learning institution. You have to experience it to understand it. Once you do, you will begin to see that knowledge doesn't always reveal itself by what happens to you, but often by what does not happen to you. It opened up a whole new way of looking at things. We must not only pay attention to what we see, but also what we do not see, and the magic lies in the "right hand not knowing what the left hand is doing."

J e r r i

As a result of Shelley's decision not to run again, I started looking around for another job as he was winding down his term of office. Someone mentioned a new television station signing on—KEMO-TV (Now KOFY), Channel 20. They were looking for a Public Service Director, and someone mentioned they might need someone with political connections. I went over, was interviewed and got the job.

During my short stay at KEMO, I helped sign the station on the air in 1968. It was here I learned about the importance of Ascertainment Forms, and how the station's license depended on filing these forms with the FCC. This was the station's way of paying back the community for their use of the airwaves that belong to the public. Also in 1968, while at the station, I produced my first television program:: *The Mel Belli Show*, and a children's program with my brother, folk singer Stan Wilson. I also was able to write and produce *White Ghetto*, a 3-part series which aired September 2, 1968, and examined some of the problems in the White community.

Then in 1969, I got a call from Terry Francois, a lawyer, and the first Black man elected to the San Francisco Board of Supervisors. He wanted me as his Administrative Assistant. Now I would get a chance to see how the other side of City Hall worked. His wife Marian and I were teenage friends, so I felt comfortable taking the job. It was while working for Francois that I had met General James Gavin. He had known Gen. Gavin and received a copy of his book, *Crisis Now*. I asked to read it, and was impressed. So when the invitation to a reception for Gavin at the Financial Club arrived, I asked to go.

While at the Board of Supervisors, I learned how the grassroots part of City government worked. Francois was on the Finance Committee and it was fascinating to see how everything must be presented and reviewed before each committee before it goes forward.

My job was to keep the Supervisor apprised of all incoming calls and matters around his constituency, answering letters from his District and seeing to it that they got their airing at City Hall. I often accompanied Francois into the Board of Supervisors Meetings, and that was really a learning experience. From the time I had landed at the door of *The Chronicle*, my job opportunities had accelerated. Except for **KEMO**, I had never had to apply for a job. I went from the *San Francisco Chronicle*, to the Mayor's office, on to a television station, then back to City Hall to work for the Board of Supervisors—all in five years. Now I was about to be on the move again.

It was 1970 and after barely a year, I got a call from **KBHK**—they wanted a Public Affairs Director and on-camera newsperson for a television program called *San Francisco Today*. I jumped at the chance. Now I could take everything I had learned at the *San Francisco Chronicle* and both sides of City Hall and use it to make my way in the broadcasting business.

It would prove to be a bumpy ride.

PART II

ARTHUR HOPPE—San Francisco Columnist-one of Jerri's first guests on SAN FRANCISCO TODAY, at KBHK. 1970. Photo courtesy of KBHK.

SAMMY DAVIS, JR. In his first interview with Jerri at KBHK, in 1972, which received a Broadcast Media Award at San Francisco State University. Second Interview was taped at Harrah's Lake Tahoe, and broadcast on KGO in 1975 on "ABOUT TIME." Photo Courtesy of KBHK.

ROCK HUDSON—Shares a laugh with Jerri. Photo taken at KBHK in 1972. Photo courtesy of KBHK.

GENERAL JAMES M. GAVIN, in a rare interview on the Vietnam War with Journalists, MICHAEL HARRIS (S.F. Chronicle), ROBERT STROUD, (UPI) and ED RADENZEL (San Francisco Chronicle), on POINT OF VIEW (KBHK), 1972. Photo courtesy of KBHK.

NICHOLAS JOHNSON, former Chairman of the FCC, discusses his book "How To Talk Back To Your Television Set." Photo courtesy of KBHK 1970.

SHIRLEY MACLAINE, talks about her trip to China with Jerri at her home in New York, for TURNABOUT, a national program designed for women, originating at KQED, 1978. Photo courtesy of KQED.

Photo of Jerri Lange in KQED Studio, photographed by John Engstead, "launching TURNABOUT, a national program for women and the men of their lives", in 1978. Photo courtesy of KQED.

CHAPTER IV

THE MAGIC OF TELEVISION

TELEVISION

It had been a long, difficult journey that had brought me high atop Nob Hill on a bright, sunny afternoon where I was being honored, at the pinnacle of my career at KQED, as "The Outstanding Broadcaster of the Year" by the American Women in Radio and Television. It was March 1, 1978. In April of 1978, I would receive San Francisco State University's most prestigious honor, the Broadcast Preceptor Award, given by the Broadcast Communication Arts Department "in recognition of signal accomplishments, leadership and adherence to the highest standards in broadcasting." The two other recipients were Walter Cronkite and Mike Wallace. It was turning out to be a banner year, but little did I know that it would mark the beginning of the end of my career in television in San Francisco.

The Broadcaster Luncheon was being held at the Fairmont Hotel and I remember wondering whether or not anyone would attend. After all, my career in broadcasting had been a controversial one, and I wasn't sure how I was perceived by my colleagues. As you will subsequently see, early in my career, I had decided to speak truthfully about what I saw lacking in the media and its response to the community. I interviewed controversial guests like Mme. W.E.B. du Bois, who had trouble being interviewed on any station, after she and her husband W.E.B. du Bois went into exile and left this country to live in Ghana.

To my great joy and surprise, more than 400 people showed up. My friends and family gathered together for a grand occasion. They even smuggled my son Ted in, without my knowledge. He was supposed to be somewhere else, unable to attend. My son, Michael, watched the corridors and brought Ted in through another entrance, where he appeared at the appropriate time. I was roasted and toasted; it was one of the happiest days of my life.

The big question that ran through my mind was, had all I had gone through been worth it? The struggle to reach the top of my profession, the battles that ensued, the sacrifices that had to be made; difficult choices leading to new frontiers and more hard work ahead? Inevitably, the answer always came back as yes. Because, you see, I was my father's child. His legacy was that it was necessary to battle to carry out one's duty to oneself, family and community.

He had a dream that brought him to San Francisco where he was honorably discharged at the San Francisco Presidio just weeks before the historic 1906 earthquake. He had given his children a dream-to excel in all that we do—reinforced by my mother. It was a dream I later handed down to my children: "Let them take away your food, your clothes, your job and your house, but don't ever let them take away your Dream. Without a dream you can't move an inch; with it you can reach the stars!" Long before I knew what I was, I knew who I was: A little Black girl who wanted the American Dream and was willing to pay the price.

It has often been said that Teddy Roosevelt walked softly and carried a big stick in order to achieve his dream. Some of us, however, are not allowed to walk softly, and society has not as yet given us a stick. So we must move through a system loaded with booby traps and land mines, hoping to make it over to the other side. Those who have made it have usually done so by charting new courses and literally bleeding through the cracks. In doing so, they have greatly enriched this country, almost against its will, and in ways yet to be discovered. But perhaps that's part of the magic that makes champions out of ordinary people.

J e r r i

As America goes through a very difficult period on its social, economic and political fronts, it may grudgingly come to realize that its nonwhite citizens—the step-children who came here with a dream, may yet become the unrealized, untapped natural resource it has barely begun to mine. When equal opportunity becomes good business for the country, then the richness of its diversity will become an asset to the world economy.

Maybe we won't need a stick after all, just a lot of faith, love and belief in a system that has yet to fulfill its destiny!

My entrance into broadcasting had been quite by accident; so it was important for me to remember this as I found myself with different goals and objectives from those of the broadcast industry in which I was involved.

I had come out of years in the white collar workplace, back into college at 36, raising three children and changing professions in mid-life. I would find myself in the newspaper business, politics, and on the board of a major broadcasting station.

I had no hidden agenda. What you saw was what you got. When you jump into an arena of game players, being up front can be most disarming at best. At worst, you can be accused of "shooting from the hip." I make no apologies; it was how I survived.

I found myself in a very different world than the one I had been accustomed to. These people played hardball. The bottom line was the dollar and the hidden agenda was control. My first misunderstanding was why anyone wanted to control others in the first place. What was the meaning of democracy unless it meant being free to believe whatever you choose to believe, as long as it doesn't interfere with others? More importantly, God gave us free will; should I expect less from others?

The energy we get by our birthright, to move through this world, express our ideas, and make our contribution as best we can, is suddenly taken over by people in power—particularly in the workplace. If you work your way up to a place that can affect public opinion, you become a target for control. I had to find out how it all plays out in the new television culture—that shapes how we think, feel and behave; that gives us new desires and dreams we have never thought of; that tells us to reach for a moon they never intend to give us. Now I needed an agenda! First I began to ask questions. This is the foundation of all learning, and many times the answers are not as important as asking the right questions. When asked correctly, the right question can pop open hidden agendas, cast light on perplexing situations, and reveal missing pieces of a puzzle.

Certain questions, however, are not welcome in the world of television. People in the industry don't have time for them. Performance usually fits a standard form: go out, get the story, bring it back and get it on the air. The one exception was KQED. It did not have a daily news program to conform to—since "Newsroom" went off the air—and was free to explore other programming. In addition it catered to an entirely different audience, and without it, television would truly be a "vast wasteland", a term used by former FCC Chairman, Newton Minnow. Thank God for PBS! Having said that, KQED still leaves much to be desired with regard to community programming, which has always been a bone of contention for air time, over airwaves that belong to the people. Time was money back in the '70's and questions of ethics never arose. What impact would this story have on the community? Where does responsibility lie? Whom does the broadcast industry serve? Who owns the airwaves? Why are people stereotyped? Why do we concentrate on the negative rather than on the positive? These were questions the industry wanted to avoid, because they were not prepared to answer them. In all honesty, broadcasters would always state on every panel I was on, that the bottom line was dollars, not information or education. People wanted to be entertained, rather than informed, they said.

I refused to buy that. I had come from a community badly in need of information about why they were in the state they were in, how they got there, and what they needed to know to get out. But, all I could ever see coming through the television tube was a continuous look at the problem, without ever seeking a solution. The television tube had become a self-fulfilling prophecy of doom, announcing what was wrong with the world but failing to tell people what they could do about it. It perpetuated negativity and would finally lead to people turning off their television sets.

Jerri

I was in hot water from day one!

This conflict would not surface immediately, because I worked at a small UHF station with a limited number of viewers. I was in public affairs, not news. My show at KBHK was *San Francisco Today*, a live, half-hour program. I gave five minutes of news, with the emphasis on interviews. The show ran for almost four years and during that time I interviewed such guests as: Former President George Bush, Sr., who was Envoy to China at that time, General James Gavin, Daniel Ellsberg, Lt. Col. Anthony Herbert, Gloria Vanderbilt, Bobby Short, Rock Hudson, Charlton Heston, David Hartman, E.G. Marshall, Sammy Davis, Jr. and the illustrious Alex Haley, to name a few. Anyone pushing a book product or controversial idea made his or her way before our cameras. I personally recruited interviews with people who were making the news.

The trouble began when I had been asked to give a speech in 1970 to the WEST Conference, a group of western educational broadcasters gathered at the Jack Tar Hotel in San Francisco.

Sherm Bazell was my first director. He encouraged me to write the "Blacks In Broadcasting" speech just as I saw it and felt it. He gave me courage to go before 400 White male educator/broadcasters and "tell it like it is." Aside from a small news item in the Sacramento Bee, it never made the news. Few people to this day, in San Francisco, ever knew I gave the speech. That's how tightly the news media is controlled. Most people will hear of the speech, only now, more than thirty years later, in this book.

I said in part: "In a world of images, we see each other through a glass darkly, if we see each other at all. We have built a technological machine that requires us to go to other lands, rich in natural resources to feed this machine. We justify our presence there by 'liberating' the people from a fate worse than death: self-determination. As the machine grows bigger, it dehumanizes us. We stand before it powerless. This machine has become so complex that it has also caused us to pollute our environment. Through ignorance and greed, the air has been rendered unfit to breathe, water unfit to drink, and food unfit to eat. We are in trouble all over the world, and on the brink of disaster at home. What kind of man destroys the thing that gives him life and creates a crisis which threatens our very existence as a species on this planet? . . . We are concerned because we want to live. This is why we find it urgent to invade the media to try to get some kind of message to you." The audience, though stunned, gave it a warm reception.

I knew when I gave that speech, even though it was not publicized, that it marked me well because the broadcasters knew I gave it. How I lasted nine more years is a mystery to me, until I realized I was much safer in a controlled setting, than as a former television personality out of reach. I was handled from that day forward, very carefully. I was given free reign to produce programs, but I could only go so far.

My next director was Buzz Anderson, who soon became a mentor and shaped my look. Buzz had an eye for style. Being one of three Black women on television, meant that you had to look good at all times. You were representing a whole race of people, breaking down barriers and stereotypes, by entering viewers living rooms in an intimate setting. I soon had a wonderful following in the Black community, and most surprisingly, the White community, who wrote letters of support. I never received a piece of hate mail during my entire nine years in television. Buzz knew what looked good on the air, and helped me select clothes that gave me a style. With Belva Davis, who was first on KPIX, Valerie Coleman Morris, second on KRON, and myself, third, on KBHK, we helped give a voice to a diverse community that was proud to see us on the air. Buzz later became an outstanding Professor in the Broadcast Communications Arts Department at San Francisco State. After Buzz left KBHK, I found a fashion designer, Vera Clanton, the first Black woman to own a boutique in San Francisco—The House of Andre. Vera dressed me until she changed her business. Much later I was able to get Helga Howie, who designed and imported beautiful clothes from Europe for her boutique. These ladies helped me find a style that is with me to this day.

Stan Burford came on board as my director after Buzz left the station. He also became a good friend and taught me a great deal about the television business. He lived and breathed it. He became KGO's Traffic Reporter, flying around the skies over San Francisco.

I found out some interesting things while at the station. During that time, stations were required by FCC regulations to give air time to the community to stay on the air. Ascertainment forms were filled out every year at the station before licensing time, enabling the community to request stories that investigate problems and possible solutions in its community. As Public Affairs Director I would invite various sectors of the community in for luncheons held at the station, and invite them to participate in programming decisions, to ensure we met the concerns of the community. Since ratings involve only news programs, far less money is invested in public affairs shows, even though it was mandatory to put them on the air. That would all change as broadcasters went back to the FCC and requested that Ascertainment be conducted every two years, then every three years, every five years, and now not at all. Now they have lifetime permission to air their programs, without going to the community.

I had been at the station barely one year but had already seen enough of television to know it was not in the best interests of bettering race relations. Most of the time, Black people were held up for ridicule on the news, in entertainment, and in the television business itself. Only one Black anchor person per station was the rule at that time. If another one was hired, the other was taken off the air. The news, to this day, is reluctant to cover any positive stories on Black people.

I remember receiving a call around 1972, from a frustrated teacher, who said that the Castlemont Castleers from Castlemont High School had just won a national competition as the best high school singing group. She called every station in the San Francisco Bay Area and asked whether they could cover these jubilant Black teenagers' return at the airport. Uniformly, the answer was negative.

During my years in television I had many Black teenagers tell me that "the press won't come out to cover anything constructive that we're involved in." (They had organized to clean up Hunter's Point, but no one wanted to cover the story). "We have to break some windows before they pay us any attention." One group got so desperate, they suggested they might do just that. They felt that once the television crew got through covering the broken windows, perhaps they could then tell them the positive story. When you give people, particularly young people, recognition only for negative acts, that is what they will engage in. This media response is perverse, reverse psychology that the media continues to practice to this day. What White America "knows" from the media is that all Black people rape, steal and cheat on welfare. When they are doing something meaningful and constructive, no one will cover the story. This is media's most insidious kind of racism. Were I White in America, I'd be a racist too, based on the information I receive through media. It is a way to keep a race of people on the bottom in the minds of others—the idea that they never make meaningful contributions to society. This act of omission is not readily identified. I saw how it was practiced willfully and unwittingly by media's managers, and it fueled a fire in me that found its oxygen in the speech I gave to the WEST Conference at the Jack Tar Hotel.

My time at KBHK was coming to an end. It had been a good run, and I learned a great deal about the broadcasting industry.

Today, much has changed at the station. It is more diverse, with more multicultural programming, like *"Black Renaissance,"* a program designed for the African American community, which first began airing while I was at KBHK.

*   *   *

After almost four years at KBHK, I was asked to join KGO, an ABC affiliate. I arrived at the station after almost three months of dickering with the producer to do a show called *About Time*. They had liked the pilot and wanted me to do a weekly show. I would have to leave KBHK. The station gave me a great sendoff, with an emotional appearance on the air, by the general manager, saying they were taking the show off the air upon my departure. After a great going-away party with our station employees and crew, I took off for KGO.

The morning I arrived, at KGO I sat at a desk outside the producer's office and waited for my first assignment. He explained that someone had forgotten to check with New York, so I was not officially hired. I was told to go home and wait for the general manager to call. I waited three weeks, using up almost all my savings. I was sitting without a job and no job to go back to, since my show *San Francisco Today* at KBHK had been taken off the air.

When I was finally called in to the office, I was told I had no show. New York had approved my position, but not the budget for the show. It was the beginning of a brand new game. The speech on "Blacks in Broadcasting" was coming back to haunt me.

I became a secretary to the man who had hired me. I sat for months doing nothing, receiving an obligatory salary, and having the distinct feeling that I was being paid to stay off the air. It is all too painful to go into detail about what happens to people in such a position, but I cringe for those I now see in pain. The objective is for you to quit.

One day as I was making my rounds of the third floor, I noticed a young Black woman with tears in her eyes. She had been crying. I decided to stop and ask her what was wrong. Her name was Claire Mack and she had a television show. It seems the producer had continually insulted her. She also said she had been told I was hired to take her place. I proceeded to tell her I not only was not hired to do her show, the program I had been hired to do was no longer in the budget, and that I had become a secretary to the producer. We immediately recognized the syndrome to divide us, and became friends. Together we organized a group of Black corporate executives to come to the station on behalf of our department—Community Affairs. The organizer outside the station was a long time friend of mine, Joe Johnson, who was then Deputy Mayor of San Francisco, under Mayor Joseph Alioto. The group made an appointment to see the General Manager, but ended up meeting with the producer. We had an airing of complaints and as a result, management seemed to back off their behavior for a while. However, it was back to business as usual before long.

Claire Mack later left KGO and went on to become Mayor of San Mateo and to host a television program on KCSM-TV.

I was finally given permission to do several segments of *About Time*, but by then the glow of working at a major television station had worn off. Being treated as a non-person in the workplace goes back to the most basic instinct to belong. You are dealing with master psychologists of human behavior who know how to push buttons to make you give in. The people who give in cannot change the system. We were in battle!

I had already learned about the importance of history and to pass on the information. So although I cannot speak for those in television today, I can speak about the need to leave a historical reference—a history that should be told because it has been replicated a thousand times throughout the nation, and in so many ways, it continues today. It is the responsibility of those who write and those in the media to tell of that history so that everyone will know it. Knowing it is knowing oneself. The necessity of self-knowledge is in the telling; those who come after you will benefit from your experience.

Throughout all this high drama, the television engineers, who handle sound, lighting and make television studios come to life, remained my friends and would do so throughout my tenure in broadcasting. A strong union made them independent so they were not under pressure to harass the talent. They were the men and women who made it all happen, so while I was in conflict with management, I was being "lit like Greta Garbo," a Hollywood legend who was instrumental in raising good lighting to an art. They were kind to me on the set, understanding the battle being waged between me and management.

I was finally allowed to do a few shows for **About Time** and another program **On the Spot**. But from then on, I was never able to shake my disillusionment with the business.

One of the programs I was asked to do was on Sickle Cell Anemia. I had read of medical concerns of Black doctors regarding the drive to target young Black children in school for testing and administering vaccinations for S.C.A. Dr. Lonnie R. Bristow, a highly respected Black physician, had done considerable research on the subject, and had written of his concerns about mandatory screening for Black children. He sent me an article he had published in the *Western Journal of Medicine*. He also sent me a copy of an article that appeared in "Reports-University of Chicago" in the Fall of 1972. It covered the concerns of a pathologist, James Bowman, about mass Sickle Cell screening programs in general, and mandatory programs in particular.

Mandatory programs are those which have been written into state law. Many years later, Dr. Lonnie R. Bristow would become the first Black President of the American Medical Association.

The television program I had been asked to host was to give a telephone number which families could call to arrange for their children to be tested for Sickle Cell. I told my producer that without further research and information, I could not do the show. He said it was not my decision whether to do the show or not-it was his. As a result, I was fired.

Soon after I was called into the front office and given a memorandum. It stated that my services were no longer required. I shook the General Manager's hand and then the hand of the assistant manager, and then thanked them both profusely and left the room. My joy at being told I no longer had a job had puzzled everyone, and spread all over the station. No one seemed to understand how much punishment I had taken and how relieved I was to finally be let go.

I sent word to my crew that I was pouring champagne on my last day at work, and hoped they could join me. As it turned out, they were detained and had to do a commercial. I was very disappointed and figured that two or three of us would have to devour the six bottles I had bought. Then one by one, the engineers came in. I had not invited them because I didn't want to get anyone in trouble. I thought it was a nice gesture. They were followed by the heads of some of the departments.

One department head of engineers said, "Jerri, we didn't want you to leave without knowing how much we think of you." He had passed me a dozen times in the corridor, and had only said "Hello."

I had found out some important things. Taking punishment and abuse may cause pain while being inflicted, but it has its rewards. You find out who you are and what you are made of; how much punishment you can take; what is important in life, and most of all, the strength and courage you find within—that changes your whole character. You will even learn to value your enemies. You need them to become who you are.

No one can ever take that away.

The KGO I watch today seems to be a totally different place. The station moved from its Golden Gate Avenue premises to their new building near the Embarcadero. The company was sold to Disney and the staff and management are new. What happened during my stay at KGO is now history.

I prepared to leave television for good. While at KBHK, I had started teaching at San Francisco State University in the Broadcast Communication Arts Department, headed by Dr. Stuart Hyde. Stu was very helpful in allowing me to make the transition to teaching, and I became a part of the adjunct faculty. It allowed me to keep my hand in the business I love, without the politics, and my students were appreciative of the factual accounts about what was going on in the television business.

By the time I finally left KGO it was 1975, which marked the International Year of the Woman. I had moderated several conferences during that year, and was invited to take a State Department sponsored tour of South America with ten other women of a group called American Women for International Understanding. As I prepared by getting shots and visas, I received a call asking if I would allow my name to be entered on a ballot to run for the Board of Directors of KQED, San Francisco's public television station? I agreed, not realizing I was putting myself right back into one of the hottest local political battles in broadcasting: "The "Battle for KQED."

Not very much had appeared in the newspapers, and as I took off for South America, the battle also took off on who would control KQED. Leslie Lipson, a reporter for *World Press*, (a national news/public affairs program formerly hosted by Casper Weinberger), also ran for the board, and we became the only on-air talent to sit on the board of a public broadcasting station. By the time I returned from my trip, the fight was going hot and heavy.

Much to everyone's surprise I garnered more than 23,000 votes, the highest ever received by a newcomer to the board. It gave me an instant constituency. It turned out to be the most interesting and informative three years of my life. I learned more about broadcasting and the power it wields than during all the other years of my career.

The crux of the issue was whether or not a station with an $11 million annual budget could maintain a news program and produce more local programming. It was the same battle all over again: the community vs. the broadcaster, for access to the airwaves. If the broadcaster is allowed to make money, then the community should have something to say about local programming, particularly a public broadcasting station, which takes money from that very same community. This became one of the main principles politicized. The community was demanding more multicultural diversity in programming. One program, *Open Studio*, which catered to the Arts, was a wonderful example of giving air time to many sections of the community. When it was taken off the air there was nothing to fill that gap. By the time I came on the Board, community activists were in the heat of battle.

Those three years taught me about hidden agendas, the role of management, sources of power, how it subtly finds its way to a target, and the power of the vote. We tried, unsuccessfully, to keep our news program *Newsroom*, on the air, and finally ended up without a news show at all. The reporters were investigative journalists originally from *The Chronicle*, and had received national attention.

In 1991, the battle erupted again, with some of the same players and a somewhat different board of directors. This time the annual budget was over $30 million dollars, (in 1999 it was $38 million).

While I may seem critical of a medium like television, it should also be noted that there are many good things coming out over the airwaves. There are always those who seem to be able to present quality programs in the midst of all the mediocrity.

One of the few local programs now on KQED is *This Week in Northern California* with Belva Davis. This program presents local stories of the day, featuring the reporters who cover the stories. A lively discussion gives the viewer a better understanding of the issues. On the national scene, *The Newshour with Jim Lehrer* gives in-depth news coverage. These two programs bring an excellent balance to the regular news programs that we usually see. We need programs that tell us what is happening around us, which usually takes more than the two minutes normally allotted to regular news stories.

KQED and PBS remain the best alternative broadcasting, along with such wonderful cable stations as the Discovery Channel, History Channel, Lifetime, and other family-oriented stations. And where would we be without C-SPAN? It just runs the camera and lets the viewers reach their own conclusion. It broadcasts every book, newsmaker, and protest without bias, and educates viewers on the inner working of Congress. Or CNN, which proves you can have an all-news network and still have an audience.

Oprah Winfrey, on ABC should be singled out for her courage in changing the format of her show, midstream, because she did not like what she saw on the television talk shows. Her current programs are uplifting and inspiring; they prove that you can present quality and still stay ahead in the ratings war. The public is the biggest winner.

While I was on the board of KQED, I was offered a show called **Womantime**. I was assured by management and our attorneys in Washington, D.C., that there would not be a conflict of interest.

Womantime was a tremendous hit and was funded for a series of programs. It was renamed **Turnabout** when it went national on PBS. It was a show designed for women and the men in their lives, an alternative to soap operas. Lane Bryant sponsored the program for one year, and when we could not get future funding, it was taken off the air.

I made plans to move on to other things.

One of those other things would be teaching in the Broadcast Communications Arts Department at San Francisco State University. This opportunity allowed me to give students an inside look at the media. I gave two Keynote speeches.

MAGIC OF TELEVISION—April 20, 1983

"You are all magicians. Because you have learned the art of producing an effect. A magician is one skilled in magic—an enchanter. You are an enchanter. That gives you power to do many things. No one can stop you from perfecting your craft, from learning necessary skills or from practicing excellence. The power to do that rests with you and if you're good, you can create magic."

Currently, magic is being performed over something that belongs to you—the Airwaves. How? It has become the new storyteller, which according to Kate Moody in her book, *Growing Up On Television,* ". . . is sanctioned by neither family, nor religion, nor school board. Its easy accessibility has stripped parents of their control."

Moody continues to say that, ". . . countless people who grew up on scary fairy tales, violent Bible stories, radio thrillers and comic and film gore are nervous about the generation now growing up on television violence. Like print, radio operates in the theater of the mind, where imagination makes the pictures. But nothing about mass media makes us more uncomfortable than the idea that the quantities of video violence produced in America and consumed around the world might be contributing to the growing epidemic of aggressive behavior."

Just as serious is her revelation that ". . . reading requires a physical technique in which the eyes move . . . and what is not generally realized is that television trains eyes not to move. Scientific studies have demonstrated that eyes move less while watching TV than in almost any other activity of daily living."

As Norman Cousins points out in his introduction of *Growing Up On Television*: "We haven't thought through the connection between the welter of images that are put into the human mind and their effect on the way the human mind functions, especially during the formative years. We haven't thought through the long-term effects on children of six hours of television viewing daily—the effects of rapid fire picture changes; the effects of discontinuation and fragmentation of ideas, thoughts, and feelings; the effects of unremitting violence and corresponding desensitization."

What about television in developed countries, where reading skills are already high? Some European countries are rejecting American imports of children's programming because it teaches them to read and write, but not to think.

This should say something very important to American parents.

A whole generation of our children have grown up under the influence of television. Some are reading before they enter the first grade. But can they think? Are they being prepared to solve problems? Are they capable of independently thinking something through? A cursory glance shows just how malleable that generation is before the throne of the television tube. It sells products, and it creates role models. It dictates behavior and alters language.

British broadcasters have described the BBC as a network which caters to a public demanding to be educated and informed, while our television caters to a public demanding to be entertained. Why are we different? And how did we get that way?

For one thing, we are constantly being fed entertainment as reality. The failure to see the thin line between serious programming and entertainment, has added to our confusion between fantasy and reality.

Then there is entertainment as entertainment. Pure entertainment, without a balance of programming dealing with human problems, can be dangerous. As Dr. Roderic Gorney put it, in a research proposal entitled *Human Survival and the Mass Media of Entertainment*: "Entertainment has served as an ancient distraction from misery, refined by the Romans into an effective method of controlling people by diverting them from reality." In other words, it releases people into the world of fantasy as a means of control.

This powerful medium should be preparing people to deal with problems of human survival. Using television to elevate the mass level of education; to better understand why we no longer have control of our lives; to use available information to solve problems, is truly using television in the public interest. But this will not be done until the public understands that the airwaves belong to the people, not to the FCC, not to the broadcaster, and not to the advertiser. They are custodians of something that belongs to you. You have the final word on what comes into your living rooms, and unless and until you, the viewing public, accept that responsibility, you will deserve what you get!

If you are setting your children before a television screen, without watching to see what they are viewing . . . if you are watching hour upon hour of programming that has no relevance to real problems facing our urban cities, educational system, government, energy crises, hunger, poverty, and environmental pollution . . . then you deserve to have your cities fail, your children remain uneducated and watch the world, as we know it, disintegrate.

For centuries, philosophers have said that the evolution of Humankind must eventually lead to a new sense of awareness about ourselves and the world in which we live, and radio and television are certainly helping to do that. We have, in fact according to Marshall McLuhan, become one big Global Village, reluctantly changing our views about our place in the scheme of things. Everything is suddenly linked, and we have become one single, living organism, trying to survive in the Universe.

We are an extension of an idea called media, a means by which we can not only look at others, but at ourselves. With this knowledge and opportunity, we need to encourage a diversity of attitudes and values so that people can intelligently choose how they shall live-rather than give them a restricted and deficient diet of very few choices. This is the balance that makes objectivity a reality.

The difficulty of all of this becomes clear when we realize that we are trying to make something work here in this country that is having trouble working all over the world: the ability of human beings to redirect their hostilities toward each other to more creative outlets. This magic tube called television, can lead us to a greater understanding of this challenge . . . of understanding ourselves and the world in which we live . . . if used properly.

The Word, now comes to us transmitted through the image of television and we wonder at its power, its magic and its imagination. It is all of these things and much more, because it controls our minds, our hearts, our behavior and how we think and feel. Its power for good is awesome and unparalleled in the history of Man. In an age of instant telecommunication, it can enable the corporate/media/ science/political and education worlds to speak not only to each other but to the community at large.

I once interviewed Historian Arnold Toynbee in London, back in 1973, and he said: "Man never learns from history, that's why we keep making the same mistakes." The problem, he pointed out, was "getting the facts." He explained how information changes and is altered as it is passed down to us through history.

It loses something in translation. It becomes His Story . . . whoever He is. In short, whoever has the power, gets to tell the story. It's all really quite simple: when power changes hands, you just rewrite history. That's the magic of power.

Hitler got to tell his story in Germany during the 1930's, by hiring a man named Joseph Goebbels, as his Minister of Propaganda. Goebbels knew that if one wants to put over a big lie, one had to be as scrupulously accurate as possible about small facts.

A student in my BCA 300 class at San Francisco State University a few years ago, submitted a paper, entitled: Joseph Goebbels and His Principles of Propaganda. He pointed out that Goebbels believed "that propaganda had to be invisible to work, especially during the early stages of the Hitler regime, while public opinion was still being formulated about the Nazi Party, and while it still made any difference what that opinion actually was.

This meant that it would not do to censor out facts and information as they were being brought to press or heard over the airwaves, but rather that the news media must only receive "the desired information to begin with." Goebbels' job was relatively easy. He had only to stage a reality and create a new world for the masses. Now that's magic!

He followed some very simple rules:

1) He practiced the art of continuous repetition.
2) The art of appealing solely to the instincts, emotions, feelings, and passions of people, while never attempting to convince intellectuals with rational arguments.
3) The art of keeping silent about uncomfortable facts . . . unless the truth reached the public in other ways.
4) The art of lying credibly, remembering that continuous repetition of a lie worked wonders.

Goebbels claimed these principles as an art, and indeed they were. He claimed that propaganda had "nothing to do with the truth."

The student concluded his paper with the startling observation that what made this all the more alarming was "that all of these techniques are now being practiced in this country to a greater or lesser degree by every form of news media."

Who are you? Who am I?—except what we perceive ourselves to be. And we perceive ourselves to be what we see, feel and hear in the images reflected all around us. Our attitude is shaped by everything we experience, but most certainly by mass media. In a sense we are all trapped by our information/mass media environment.

One television producer was heard to joke one day, "what's happening around the world today, that isn't happening-because we aren't covering it?" Now, that's power!

Power, however, doesn't always mean freedom. Some People think they are free because they can move about. But that's just linear movement. Freedom is much more than that. Freedom means exempt from subjection to the will of others; being at liberty, not in confinement; not encumbered, affected or oppressed.

Make no mistake about it, you are dealing with Magic. The hand has always been quicker than the eye, and the media is quicker than that. It's a hook, it picks you up and never lets you down, and we get caught up in the glamour of it all. But you have a chance to change all that, because freedom also means finding a torch and lighting your way out of darkness, the torch so bravely carried by our forefathers.

We have the capacity, through satellite, to permit a universal dialogue throughout the world and even into outer space. Telecommunications can ensure harmonious development by bringing people closer together and contribute to the establishment of universal peace. How do we do this? By making television more responsible to the public it has been mandated to serve. It will not be easy.

We must learn to monitor television programs. If you plan to gripe about the manipulation of the television tube and poor programming to station managers, you'd better have your facts ready. How many hours of programming contained violence or racism? At what time did these programs occur? The Surgeon General who wrote the explosive report on the impact of television violence on human beings, *Television and Growing Up: The Impact of Televised Violence*, indicated that violent programs on TV can have harmful effects on large groups of children. He is no longer in office. The report, however, is . . . and still available for people to read. Read it. Find out what action was taken after this basic research was done.

We must respond to stereotypes depicted on television. Stereotypes bring on racism and racism invites violence. Lack of understanding creates fear. People are afraid of each other. How can we solve our mutual problems while dealing with fear just because we are in each other's presence? It is important to see to it that the television industry depicts America as it really is: a multi-racial nation where diversity is a strength, not a weakness. Television writers are discouraged from writing any scripts depicting nonwhites and women as human beings rather than cartoons, or placing values on anything not grounded in crass materialism. We have therefore produced a society of people who fail to see the positive contributions of minorities or women, not only to this nation, but to the world.

Learn to ask questions. Does a constant diet of violence on television help build a non-violent people? Is television helping to promote crime and racism in our urban cities? Do people act out what they see on television? What can be done to create an audience that will watch non-violent shows?

We have just faced the shocking reality that the earth has served notice it will no longer continue to provide unlimited natural resources that we have taken for granted all of our lives, while we continue to destroy and pollute the environment. Are we developing programs providing possible solutions or just examining the problem?

In a society where it is becoming more and more evident that automation will take over most of the jobs now held by people, no one is being prepared for changes in the work ethic. Only the elite will be working full time. Unemployment in large numbers is shaking the foundation of our homes and faith in ourselves.

Are we gathering information and informing people of the coming "leisure" revolution, and what the impact of our changing work ethic will have on this society?

Many intelligent people are stagnating and vegetating in our urban cities and suburbs, while loneliness, alienation and the generation gap contribute to alcoholism, drugs and suicide. Are we dealing intelligently with these problems? Are we giving people information about alternative lifestyles that can change and enrich their lives?

Who is responsible for creating and maintaining the "public taste?" WE ARE. We decide-ultimately-what goes out over the airwaves, by assuming responsibility for the broadcasters' choice of programming.

We have allowed television broadcasters to pander to the lowest mental capacity and animal instincts in the human psyche, feed people more of the same, then expect them to choose something totally alien to their experience. We have allowed to develop a generation of people unable to appreciate first class non-violent programming which is, perhaps, the saddest chapter in our history of television.

It is also a serious indictment of the television industry's failure to use this powerful medium as an influence capable of changing attitudes, values and behavior of millions of people to a higher level of human development. This failure to assume responsibility for our actions can lead to mind control and censorship, if we fail to exercise our rights as owners of this nation's airwaves.

We must take back our airwaves. The FCC has clearly mandated that the airwaves belong to the public, and that the public should have some input on what goes out over the air. Until the public accepts this responsibility, broadcasters will continue to look to the bottom line as their guide.

Intelligent use of television can change our image of ourselves as people, corporations and organizations and help us decide, once and for all, how we intend to view ourselves. We must turn our talents toward problem solving. We already know what the problems are.

The world will not change until we decide to change it. Our responsibility should be to begin that change.

But some of us are slow to accept change, and if we are to play a meaningful role, we must *now* begin to translate new values, meanings and a different view of life to the world. We have to reach out to the world in order to communicate ourselves to others. There is a dichotomy between what we *are* and how others *view* us. *And we must close that gap.*

ETHICS—March 31, 1982

In an age of instant telecommunications, we are not really communicating. "We" meaning the corporate/media/science/education/political worlds, as well as the community at large. We form highly specialized groups who speak only to each other.

This lack of communication has caused considerable problems for the world as it is perceived by the community, and the way many of us perceive society at large. There is a need for dialogue, between corporations, our public institutions and the community. Our growing interdependence upon each other in the coming decade will be a reality by the year 2000. Even competitors may have to sit down and discuss societal needs and solutions. Before this can be done, however, in any meaningful way, we must discuss the question of ethics. Where better to start than with our youth, tomorrow's leaders, and with you, the educators, given the task and the challenge to point the way. We can affect their choices by beginning to communicate, relate and interrelate; to express, create and burst forth with new ideas.

Why ethics—after all this time?

I ran across an article recently on a author named Sissela Bok, discussing her new book, published last Spring, entitled: *"Lying: Moral Choice In Public and Private Life."* I was not only fascinated by the subject, but by its timeliness. Dr. Bok is the wife of Derek Bok, President of Harvard College, daughter of Gunnar Myrdal, and teaches a course at Harvard entitled "Ethics and Decision-making in Medicine." She began by doing articles on ethical questions regarding lying in medicine, which eventually launched her into a much broader four year study of lying by other professionals: businessmen, governments, and parents, for what they sometimes believed to be very good reasons.

"I came to feel very strongly," said Dr. Bok, "that they do injure themselves, much more than they know. They injure their integrity.

And because they know they are not entirely to be trusted, they can no longer be sure that other people don't suspect that too. People who are lied to are harmed because they are manipulated. They are led to make choices on the basis of false information. Their choices might well be different if they knew they were being lied to. Once you lose that kind of confidence and trust," continues Dr. Bok, "you begin to think that professionals to whom you turn, are trying to manipulate in this way. Then it is very hard to regain the confidence that has been lost."

Dr. Bok says that since the beginning of the 20th Century, teaching of ethical questions almost vanished from the general curriculum of American Universities, and she often had to go back to the Middle Ages and the classical period to find real philosophical debates on the choices a person should make when wondering whether to lie or tell the truth.

"Just in the last five years or so a tremendous interest in professional ethics has sprung up," says Dr. Bok. This, she predicts, will result in long standing professional codes of ethics being revised and new codes written. Some professions now have no codes at all. "Today," she continues, "students want to talk about and study ethics. And some universities are requiring it. In schools of law, medicine, journalism, in all kinds of training areas, courses in professional ethics are coming into being. In the last five years we have had more writing on the subject than in this whole century put together."

So there you have it. Ethics. Something we've lost and are trying to find again. And I don't think we will find it until we face a few hard realities about ourselves as a culture and a people . . . until we usher in new ideas and be honest about ourselves-our strengths as well as our weaknesses.

That this should be so painful to the rest of society, is a mystery that has plagued creative souls since the beginning of time. It is as if there is some mysterious, invisible force waiting at the gates of the City, daring you to enter, with an independent thought. Presenting a new idea is like entering a dark room and reaching for the light switch-not knowing whether you will light up the room or be blown to bits!

But we must press onward, because human beings either move forward and grow-or stagnate and die. We are all here I hope, because we have chosen to grow.

What I'd like to talk about today is where we're going. We are sitting in the midst of the most powerful force for good in the world, a force capable of solving some of the most crucial and complex problems of our time: literacy, population growth, the environment, the energy crisis, and human rights, to name a few. We have the capacity-through satellite-to permit a universal dialogue throughout the world and even in outer space. By bringing people closer together, telecommunications can ensure harmonious development and contribute to the establishment of universal peace. It is no wonder, then, on the brink of these great events, that we should discuss ethics.

With the West under increasing fire to report developments in the Third World in an unbiased manner, we media are on trial. Those of us who are minorities were not surprised by that charge at all, since we are still trying to create the same kind of sensitivity here in the United States. I think one of the messages they'd like the West to report for instance, is how some of the underdeveloped nations are using the medium of television. In some instances, more creatively than we are. In countries where illiteracy is very high, television is used as an educational tool. In Nigeria, for example, it is used to bring literacy to a country where an estimated 250 languages and dialects are used. And to rebuild and unify a country.

I recently visited several African countries, and found a vast, sprawling continent, blessed with the richness of natural resources, but nevertheless, plagued with the same problems of the developed nations-as it enters the modern world: problems of pollution, population control, the environment, political, social and cultural change. Despite well known tribal differences, however, Africans are getting together to solve their mutual problems, particularly those of the environment. I attended an African Regional Workshop on Environmental Education for Adult Education in Nairobi. The first of its kind, it was attended by professionals and environmental experts from Nigeria, Ghana, Zambia, Botswana, Tanzania, Uganda, Sierra Leone, Gambia, Swaziland and Kenya. African children under 4 years of age, are dying of lung disease because of air pollution. There has been very little exchange of information with the West, because hardly anyone knew the Conference was being held. The only thing we hear about Africa is how incapable they are of solving their problems without colonial rule.

The classrooms in Dakar are sparse to say the least. They have none of the sophisticated learning tools we have here in this country. Some of the children are dressed in clean rags, but they are learning mathematics and speak four languages, (French, English, Wolof, (their tribal tongue), and at least one other tribal language). They are planning to become doctors, lawyers, educators, engineers. They plan to go abroad to Universities for advanced studies (in London, Paris), and return to their countries to serve their people. What are the magic ingredients? Motivated students and dedicated teachers. It's a story you won't see on television, or read in the newspapers. So much for unbiased news reporting!

But nowhere has media failed us more than in the field of human relations. The stereotypes presented on television have to be seen to be believed. The producers of these shows are quick to call it "entertainment." Is the practice of presenting women, blacks, and other minorities in controlled situation comedies, designed to present them as less than human? If so, the rest of society can write them off. Certainly they don't suffer as much, hurt as much, feel as much or get angry as much, as other human beings. They don't love, because they aren't real. They are cartoons, and we are not to take them seriously.

This practice of stereotyping contributes to subtle forms of racism and discrimination throughout this country. But in the Midwest, where there are very few minorities, it becomes even more dangerous. These people rarely see minorities, and the only contact they do have is through programs they see on television, as entertainment. Needless to say, they believe what they see.

The responsibility of media should be to destroy rather than create stereotypes. It should prepare people to respect their cultures, and feel comfortable with people who look different than they do. The failure to do this has hurt the majority of white Americans as much as it has hurt its minorities. Racism often paralyzes whites to deal in international affairs. In our relationships around the world, failure to interrelate with non-white people has been evident everywhere. The failure of our Vietnam involvement, was first in stereotyping the Vietnamese people, and then underrating them. In a changing world this can only lead to misunderstanding and chaos. When racism begins to stand in the way of trade relations, emerging new governments and shifting power into non-white hands . . . then stereotyping becomes very costly indeed. Ingrained racism may then cause a loss of badly needed natural resources, trade agreements and economic and political stability abroad. Let us not let the international parade pass us by!

On the domestic front, racism invites violence. Lack of understanding creates fear. People are afraid of each other. How can we solve our mutual problems of diminishing natural resources, while dealing with fear of each other's presence. It is ironic that white Americans have also been the victims of their own stereotyping. While in Europe, many people asked how I could live in such a violent country, where everybody packed guns. They see Americans as the most violent people on this earth, based on the television shows we send them!

Former *San Francisco Examiner* television critic, Dwight Newton, writing in his column entitled "The Shame of American TV," wrote: "In England, the Netherlands, Belgium and France, I found that very few of our prestige specials reach Europe. Some of our situation comedies are quite popular. The most common American products are crime and violence programs. The American image on European television has become a soiled and sullied image. To the average European viewer, we are shaping up as the United States of crime. Maybe we are."

Lord Lew Grade, owner of England's commercial television network, and many of its theaters, has a few answers. Asked by reporters why such prestigious programs of his *(Long Days Journey Into Night, Hamlet, The Merchant of Venice, and Antony and Cleopatra,)* attracted such embarrassingly low ratings in America, Lord Grade replied: "American networks don't educate their viewers . . . they saturate the public with crime shows and comedy shows. Viewers become used to nothing but that diet, night after night. Since that's all they know, that's all they want. People here believe in a balanced diet. Besides the series programs, we televise six or seven dramas a week. Every week."

We live in very troubled times. In the next few years, today's students will make their entrance on the world scene, as our future leaders. We haven't left them much of a legacy. Our students aren't writing poetry, they're making atom bombs . . . and bragging about it. And what's even worse, if they are writing poetry, we're not hearing about it because it isn't news. Society tells them to look out for No. 1. About the only place people are generously rewarded for teamwork is on the football fields or on the basketball court. It is a sad commentary on the nobility that once was ours.

What happened to the time when we produced men who shouted, "Give me liberty or give me death?" Are we too late to recapture that moment . . . to regain our courage to build a better world? I haven't the slightest doubt that we can. History isn't made by civilizations. Sometimes it moves forward on the contribution of just one man or one woman who dares to enter that city with an idea, armed with the courage and dedication to carry it off. You and I reap the benefits.

CHAPTER V

BACKSTAGE/ON CAMERA

MALCOLM X

Malcolm X was one of my first interviews—long before I entered the world of television. In 1964, I was part of a 3-unit Sunrise Semester course for San Francisco State University taped at KPIX. Among other illustrious speakers, would be Aileen Hernandez, who later became President of the National Organization for Women and a leading activist in the International Women's Movement; and Horace Cayton, who became my mentor and whom I write about later in this book.

Malcolm X would prove to be one of the most important persons I would ever meet. At the time, no one knew the incredible impact he would have on the Black community. My son Michael would recreate his speeches, "Message To The Grassroots" and "The Ballot or The Bullet" many years later. I remember how surprised I was at Malcolm X's demeanor. This was not the fiery, rabble-rousing terrorist I had heard about, but a quiet, almost sensitive looking man, who looked scholarly in his glasses, which perfectly framed a pair of soulful eyes. He looked directly at you when he spoke. He spoke softly. He had two bodyguards with him.

It had taken a long time for the Black community to embrace Malcolm. He had been misunderstood in so many ways, because of how he was covered in the media, and it seemingly took years for mainstream Blacks to accept and understand where he was coming from. But subsequent years since his assassination, we have seen his reputation grow to icon status. As many of our civil rights gains began to disappear, young people in particular began to follow his teachings. He is now widely accepted by the older generation as well, as his prophetic predictions materialize. *The Meeting* is a play about a fictional meeting between Dr. Martin Luther King, Jr. and Malcolm X; it aired on PBS and is now performed in theatres and schools around the country. My son Michael, who bears an uncanny resemblance to Malcolm, started out performing his speeches and went on to perform in *The Meeting*, portraying Malcolm, while my other son Ted, played Dr. King in one performance (it has continued with James Brooks as Dr. Martin Luther King, Jr.).

If there has been a high point in my life, it was that evening, watching my two sons on stage portraying two of our twentieth century's greatest advocates for people of color all over the world. Michael has also produced a documentary on the life of Malcolm X, showing all of the people who visit his gravesite every year on the date of his death—from all over the world. It is narrated by Ossie Davis, reciting his electrifying eulogy on "Our Black and Shining Prince". You will never read about it in the newspapers, magazines or see it on television. News is managed, and let us not ever forget it.

GENERAL JAMES M. GAVIN

I was given a longer, in-depth evening program called *Point of View* at KBHK. One of my first guests was General James M. Gavin. I had first heard his name when I worked at the *San Francisco Chronicle*, and wanted to put together a program with Carl Rowan, then head of the USIA. They were both Ambassadors—Rowan in Finland and Gavin in Paris. Unfortunately, the program with the two of them never came off.

I had been impressed with General Gavin since I read his book, *Crisis Now*, and was astounded to find a military man who spoke of peace. Gavin had been the first outspoken opponent of the Vietnam War when everyone else in the military was for the war. It took courage, and he was willing to pay the price. When he later came to San Francisco as Chairman of the Board of the Arthur D. Little Company, and on the occasion of the publication of his book, I wanted to meet him just to shake his hand. A reception for him was held at the Financial Club and I attended. It was there, that day, that we became friends. He became a mentor and a major force in my life. He taught me to have courage, how to fight and how to stand up for what you believe in. He said that to win the game of life, one must become a military strategist, because the game is a battlefield, strewn with land mines, just waiting to go off at one wrong move. One must, therefore, learn to establish beachheads, engage the enemy in divertive action and know when to move forward and when to retreat. When I realized that I was talking to the man who headed Research and Development for the Pentagon, and who had created the 82nd Airborne Division that landed in Normandy on that historic day, ending World War II, I listened very, very carefully.

When we put together the program, an incident occurred which gave me further insight into how news managers control what we see. My set included a round table which would seat me with my guest and visiting reporters. The station had no idea I would bring on such a powerful guest as General James Gavin. We did the program and it was scheduled to run the following Sunday. Somewhere during the week, the videotape got lost on its way upstairs for editing. They ran another show in its place. I was outraged! I immediately called Charles Gould, publisher of the *San Francisco Examiner*, and Dwight Newton, television critic of the same paper, and told them that a very important program on the Vietnam War had been misplaced in the station. Gould put on some pressure, and Dwight Newton noted in his column that the station had lost the tape. The tape was found and aired the following Sunday, with an apology from the station. That was just the half of it.

The next day I was called in and shown a diagram of my new set that was being built for *Point of View*. My guest would sit by himself facing me, my back would be to the camera, and reporters would be sitting on the side asking questions. It was bizarre. It turns out that the shape of a table, which is so important in negotiations, also sends signals to the world at large. King Arthur had created the round table for equals, and the station would not have me sitting and talking to a U.S. Army General and reporters as an equal. I used that set until my departure from KBHK. My set on *San Francisco Today* remained the same, so many people did not notice the change. For me, it was another eye-opener.

GENERAL TANG ZI CHANG

In 1970, I interviewed another General very much like James Gavin. General Tang Zi Chang was a General in the Army of General Chiang Kai-Shek, head of the Nationalist government in Taiwan. We met when he came on my show to display his war paintings. He had left China, disgusted with war and had chosen to live a life of peace, painting the horrors of war. We became friends and he gave me three autographed, first edition copies of his books, *Principles of Conflict; Wisdom of Dao* and the *Poems of Tang*. He was a descendant of the Tang Dynasty and had attended schools all over the world.

At lunch one day, he said: "The highest developed human beings on earth are the North American Indians." He recounted how unfortunate it was that they were almost destroyed, but luckily their culture was still intact; he said that one day we would all learn from them. I found this a very stimulating observation from one of his high standing. He, like Benjamin Franklin and Thomas Jefferson, also understood the beauty and spiritual nature of the American Indian culture.

The three books he gave me were self-published. They were bound in rich embroidered silk, each a different color: royal blue, dark green and beige. Each was placed inside a beautiful book cover, with a photograph of Gen. Tang Zi Chang and an extensive biography.

Whenever I show my silken treasure, people are amazed, saying: "Jerri, this man gave you the world."

SHIRLEY GRAHAM DUBOIS

I have always been an admirer of W.E.B. DuBois, so when I got a chance to interview his wife, Shirley Graham DuBois, I was thrilled.

She was quite a person in her own right, and helped her husband in so many ways. She was granted a six weeks visit to the United States. She and her husband W.E.B. DuBois had left the country and settled in Ghana. Once there, President Kwame Nkrumah gave them a house, car and driver, so that DuBois could finish his great work, *Encyclopedia Africana,* a book on the words used to enslave Black people, and compilation of new words that would free them. When the coup went down in Ghana, DuBois's work was confiscated and he was arrested. Many years later I met the minister of culture from Ghana who told me they had recovered the work and finished the *Encyclopedia.* The work was published by *Encyclopedia Brittanica* under the name *Africana: The Encyclopedia of the African American Experience.* After DuBois's death, Shirley moved to Egypt, where she resided when she came on the program. She told me about the confiscation of the work off-camera, since her trip here was controversial. However, we did talk about how well she and her husband had been treated in Ghana before the coup, and how happy she was to be living in Egypt. She spoke of how close she lived to the Nile River and what it meant to the African people. She said the Nile was the source of all life in Africa, and that as long as it flowed, Africa would survive. She was very inspiring and it was one of the high points of my interviews at KBHK.

ALEX HALEY

Another guest was Alex Haley. At the time he was working on a major book tracing his ancestry. We now know it as *Roots.* We did an hour long show and Alex revealed how many years of research it had taken him to do the book and how important it was for all people to search for their roots. I am not sure that even he was prepared for the staggering success that followed.

I am sure many people have various stories about Alex Haley, and I would like to share one. Alex was writing his book just a few stories above me; we both lived in the same apartment complex on the Embarcadero. I called him one evening to tell him my son, Ted, was flying in to avoid two ladies who were fighting over him at the time. Knowing very little about how men can avoid such situations, particularly when they are in the limelight, I asked Alex could he come down and counsel Ted on what to do.

Ted was coming in late in the evening. As busy as he was, it was close to midnight when Alex showed up. He came in and spent almost an hour with Ted in a private conversation about the pitfalls of becoming famous and the attraction of women to a rising star. I shall be forever grateful for Alex's kindness to me and Ted. He was a very soft-spoken, warm, kind and generous man.

ARNOLD TOYNBEE

While still at KBHK, Henry Urrows, an editor for *Educational Television Magazine*, a national magazine on television, asked if he could use the "Blacks In Broadcasting" speech on his editorial page. A report of the speech was published in the January 1971 issue of the magazine. Ironically, it was a reprint of that article that got me in to see Arnold Toynbee in London, in September of 1971. It was my first trip abroad, and I decided not to waste the opportunity.

I asked General Gavin to send letters to the London and Paris Embassies. He did so. By the time I arrived in London, a note was in my box at the hotel, asking me to contact Mr. C.J. Davies of the Central Office of Information in London upon my arrival.

When I arrived at the COI, I was warmly greeted and taken upstairs, introduced to two more officers and then we all sat for tea. The table was complete with nameplates, tiny British and American flags and beautiful china. As they poured tea, each officer asked me what I would like to see. I told them my son, Ted, was an aspiring young actor and wanted to enroll in the Royal Academy of Dramatic Arts, where he could study under Sir Laurence Olivier, as a student of Shakespeare. I asked to visit the BBC, the *London Times* and *The Observer*, possibly talking to some of the journalists there. I also asked for a list of other places I should see, and, of course, a guide to the best plays in town. But my last request caused quite a stir. I wondered whether it was possible to see Professor Arnold Toynbee. I purposely saved that request for last, knowing it would be the most difficult to grant. However, I was not prepared for their reactions. "No one sees

Professor Toynbee," someone said. "He has been ill; he had a heart attack in Japan and his wife has not been well. He is currently working on a very important work and shouldn't be disturbed."

"I've been turned down before," I said. "Could we just ask? If he says no, my feelings will not be hurt." They agreed to think about it.

They escorted me downstairs and said a letter would be in the "post" in a couple of days, giving me all the information I needed, as well as the dates and times of appointments they had arranged.

I had been an admirer of Toynbee since reading an article in which he stated that the true winners of World War II were not the United States and Russia, but Japan and Germany. They would not have the enormous expense of maintaining occupation forces in other countries, therefore, they could concentrate on developing their economy and possibly accomplish through trade what they could not win through war. His prophecies had turned out to be all too true. Japan lost Pearl Harbor, but until the recent stock market crash in Japan, Japanese owned almost every hotel in Honolulu and through acquisition of land, much of the economy. Germany has remained a world power, their standard of living is high and the German mark strong. Toynbee seemed to have a clear view of the spoils of war and explained why man never learns from history. He never sounded pompous, using history as a lesson that an average person, like me, could understand. I wanted very much to meet him.

Exactly two days later, a letter came, advising me that I was to see several people at the BBC, a journalist at the *London Times*, and advising whom I was to see at RADA. Also enclosed was an address for Professor Toynbee's country home. I was to write him for an appointment at his apartment in London. I wrote the letter and enclosed a copy of the reprint "Blacks in Broadcasting."

Two days later, I was awakened by a phone call early in the morning. A voice spoke, hurriedly giving his name, asking if I could come for a ten o'clock appointment the next morning. I said yes, suddenly realizing that I was actually talking to Arnold Toynbee! It was a dream come true. I was beside myself; I hurriedly called Mr. Davies and explained that I couldn't keep my other appointments. "Why not?" he asked. "Because I'm going to see Arnold Toynbee," I replied.

"You're what?" he asked, plainly shocked. "I'm going to see Arnold Toynbee," I repeated excitedly. "How did you manage that?" he continued. "I just did what you told me to do. I wrote him a letter saying I was a visiting American journalist who admired his work and would like to see him." I paused and then said, "I also enclosed an article I wrote."

"What article?" he shot back.

"Oh, just a reprint of a speech I gave back in San Francisco last year." I continued.

"Well, I'd like to hear it," he said.

"It's awfully long to read over the telephone," I countered.

"I've got time," he said.

I then proceeded to read the entire speech, over the phone and when I finished, he asked me to please keep him posted on the meeting and that he would get busy changing my appointments at the BBC and the *London Times*.

The next day I headed for Arnold Toynbee's apartment house, and I remember going up several floors in one of those birdcage elevators that you see in all the British movies. (As a matter of fact, I began to feel as though I was really in a British movie). Was all this actually happening to me? Was I really going to see Arnold Toynbee? What was I going to say when I met him? I trembled at the thought. Before I could answer the questions, I found myself standing in front of a door. I knocked and the door was opened by the world's greatest living historian, a man who had become a legend in his own time. At 82 years old, he had snow white hair, slightly bent, and wore a hearing aid. In spite of all this, he was alert and for the first time in my life, I could actually see energy in a human face. It seemed as though he had pulled all of his remaining forces together to finish his last work. His immediate impact was overwhelming and I knew without question, as I gazed into his sparkling eyes, that I was in the presence of a formidable intellect. I liked him immediately.

He was working on a trilogy that included Greek and Roman history. As we talked, I felt as if we had known each other all of our lives. He was pleasant, absolutely knowledgeable, and easy to talk to.

He was not condescending and proved once again, that when a person is not threatened by your presence, there is no need to belittle you or make you feel uncomfortable. A benefit of experiencing his great intellect was that thereafter I had a model against which to compare others. I knew by his warm regard and respect for me, that I would not be intimidated by lesser men.

As it turned out, he was not seeing me as a Black woman from America, but a piece of a puzzle, a member of a race of people with a long history in another part of the world, transplanted through slavery to that continent. I was part of a historical reference he could bring up to date and he knew, from reading my article, that regardless of the questions he posed, I would tell him the truth. What I did not know at the time was that he was working on a new book, with Daisaku Ikeda, president of Soka Gakkai, a Buddhist lay organization, one of the largest in Japan. The book, *The Toynbee-Ikeda Dialogue-Man Himself Must Choose*, was published in 1976. One of the chapters discussed the environment and the oneness of man and nature, a subject which I had touched on in my article which sparked his interest. We spent a fascinating two hours talking about the historical past of all people, the true origin of races, and I sat amazed as he explained how one flows into the other.

We compared the English-Belfast situation to racism in the United States, the interment of the Japanese in the United States during World War II, and how we are all "victims and prisoners of our historical past," as he put it. He showed me the original volumes of *A Study of History*, which lined his study. It was an enormous work. He said that his wife had been a tremendous help to him in researching the project.

He also showed me notes from his work in progress. His study was a mass of spread-out papers, reflecting a scholar in the midst of research and writing; books were open for referencing. I was struck by the simplicity of the entire apartment and study. Most British professionals have modest apartments in London, since most of them keep homes in the countryside. Their London apartments are kept as workplaces or home offices. Toynbee seemed to be working against the clock, to finish a massive study of Greek and Roman history. All the energy I felt in that room reflected that urgency.

I told him I was tired of fighting the forces of power, and had decided to become the very best human being I knew how to be, then go around the world looking for others. To my surprise, he said, "Well, Jerri, that's the answer after all, isn't it?"

He graciously allowed me to call an end to our visit. (He was to see a group of Japanese businessmen the following day). We said goodbye.

By the time I reached my hotel, Mr. Davies had called with my new appointments, different people from those originally scheduled. It seems the appointment with Toynbee had caused quite a stir, and I didn't know why. My first appointment was with the Foreign Editor of the *London Times*, E.C. Hodgkin. He was a delightful man. During our long talk about my London visit, he said: "I heard you saw the old man. How does he look these days?" I told him he looked very well, considering his age and his heart attack. Mr. Hodgkin then invited me to spend the weekend at Great Missenden, his country home, with his wife Nancy and himself. That weekend was a great experience. Perhaps the beauty of the English countryside has something to do with the fact that English writers live so long. I walked on what seemed to be a soft, velvet carpet throughout the countryside; it was the piling up of leaves that fell and gathered from year to year and you almost bounced along as you walked. How much history, I wondered, lay beneath my feet. Everyone grew roses, tended their gardens and lived simply.

We took a side trip to Little Missenden, where I entered a small church and saw carvings in the wooden pews that had been there for centuries. People rode about on bicycles; families had lived together for hundreds of years. This was a community where people knew and cared for each other. If this was what humankind could become, warm and friendly and unafraid of each other, then the future was worth fighting for.

It was at the BBC, at a four-hour lunch with the top producer, that the cat was let out of the bag, as it were. After some discussion about my perceptions of London, the producer asked the same question "I heard you saw Toynbee. How does he look?"

"Why is everyone asking about Arnold Toynbee?" I asked. "He writes a column in the *London Observer*, doesn't he?"

"Yes," he replied, "But no one has seen him for almost five years."

I had been running around London with the most important interview in years and didn't know it. "Well," I continued, "he's seeing a delegation of visiting Japanese businessmen, so obviously he's seeing somebody."

The following year my name was put up for the Federal Communications Commission by the National Women's Political Caucus. I wrote to Toynbee and asked him for a letter of recommendation. On his stationery of the Royal Institute of International Studies, London, England, he wrote a beautiful letter stating that he based his recommendation on the "work we did together on your recent trip to London." Only a very kind man would write such a letter for someone who spent all of two hours in his presence. The letter was framed and is in the archives of the Berkeley Historical Society.

The question of interviewing Arnold Toynbee would later be controversial because of his comments in "A Study of History." Toynbee had stated that Blacks, as a race, had made no "contribution" to civilization. I did not know this before I asked for the interview. Since the speech on "Blacks in Broadcasting" certainly indicted racism in the United States and bias in the media, he certainly knew where I was coming from.

He was gracious, answered all of my questions and treated me with respect. If he still believed what he had written so many years ago, he showed no signs of it to me. My father taught me to always talk to people who had opposite viewpoints, because you might learn something, and there would always be an exchange of information. For instance, regardless of our differences, the dominant culture continues to borrow from our culture because it is rich with creativity. Black energy romps through this country like a bull in a china shop: in music, dance, sports, language and style.

So, I am glad I went to the interview with an open mind and a willingness to understand history. I was not disappointed. If you truly believe there is a higher force always working in your favor, meeting with someone controversial can still open up a door to knowledge. I am sure diplomats and peacemakers experience this all the time.

As I look back, I realized that Toynbee opened a whole new world to me. History had come alive, and if you don't know who you are, or where you come from, you are locked in a world you may never understand. It would also explain why Alex Haley's **Roots** struck such a chord with all races. We are all trying to find our way back home.

Toynbee's positive response to my remark about becoming a better human being was perhaps the turning point in understanding that if we are to change the world at all, we must first begin with ourselves.

The other discovery was that no matter how tightly a door is closed, you never know when it might open.

Meeting him had been another one of those lucky breaks that had come my way and affected my life. I was beginning to find a pattern of my life. Someone said, "When the student is ready the teacher appears." The teacher changes your direction, arms you with knowledge, then lights the way.

SAMMY DAVIS, JR.

The most important and newsworthy interview I did at KGO was my interview with Sammy Davis, Jr.

I first met Sammy Davis, Jr. when he came to do an interview on *San Francisco Today*, at KBHK. He had helped my son, Ted Lange, launch *Golden Boy* at the University of Santa Clara where Ted was then a Director-in-Residence. Davis didn't know Ted but had heard he was having difficulty staging the play, so he sent his manager over with the original script from the London version of the play. The gesture helped tremendously. He also sent a long telegram to Ted on opening night. Davis had performed many such acts of kindness which were never made public.

The big interview with Sammy Davis, Jr., however, would come when I worked at KGO, an ABC affiliate. He had hugged President Nixon, and the Black Community was in an uproar. They thought that such an act was sheepish, tommish and degrading to the Black Community, during a time of great social and racial upheaval. Among the most militant Blacks, he was considered the poster boy for Black acculturation and accepted White dominance. He felt the rage from the Black Community and it touched him deeply.

Davis was totally caught off guard, and felt he deserved to give his side of the story. This was big news, and from the point of view of a journalist, media had a responsibility to give him equal time. He wanted a chance to respond. My producer and I arranged an exclusive interview with him and flew with a crew to Harrah's, Lake Tahoe.

When we arrived, something told me to throw away my pre-arranged questions. My producer and I had discussed the questions on the plane, he felt that we might have to end up winging it, and he was right. Davis had taken so much abuse, that he just wanted to tell his side of the story. I decided to hang loose. All I had to do was clear my throat and off he went!

In one of the most candid half hour interviews I can recall, he spoke in great pain about the Black response to his action. He said the media had never showed the preceding long introduction in which President Nixon gave a glowing account of Davis, what he meant to the entertainment business, describing his many acts of kindness and making the observation that he could not be bought. It was an extraordinary tribute. Sammy was so overwhelmed by the words of a President lauding him as a great human being, that he rushed over and hugged him. He explained that it was a natural reaction to all the kind things being said about him in public. He never thought to hold back, or consider how it would look to others, particularly the Black Community. He went on to say how many thousands of dollars he gave annually to the United Negro College Fund and talked about all the other ways he had tried to help others. He concluded by saying how much he loved his people, then broke into tears on camera. There were about thirty people in the room, including his manager/musical arranger, George Rhoades, and his wife; everyone was astonished; you could hear a pin drop. I quickly ended the interview with a quote from Lorraine Hansberry's play, **Raisin in the Sun**: "Before you judge a man, you must consider the valleys as well as the mountains." I went over to him where he was standing in a corner of the room and wrapped my arms around him. We stood there for about five minutes, holding each other. Everybody in the room wept silently.

These are the rare, poignant moments in television which can be rich and rewarding.

Back in San Francisco, the management of KGO was ecstatic! There was talk of the Emmy we would surely get for one of the best interviews ever. I remember all the excitement and joy of the evening of the Emmy Awards, as everyone stopped by our table and said, "Next year, we get ours for Sammy." I had already received the prestigious Broadcast Media Award from San Francisco State for the previous interview I had done with Sammy Davis, Jr. at KBHK. By the time the Emmys rolled around for the dramatic and tearful KGO interview, however, time had passed and the station and I were at odds; the show was never entered for consideration.

The *Turnabout* program on PBS had pleasant moments and good interviews. Where else could I have interviewed both Shirley Temple Black on the West Coast and Shirley MacLaine on the East Coast, and put them together into one show called "The Two Shirleys?"

SHIRLEY TEMPLE BLACK

When we arrived at Shirley Black's home in Woodside, she greeted us warmly, ushered us into her living room filled with African Art from her years as U.S. Ambassador to Ghana. It had some lovely family heirlooms, as well. A very special piece belonged to her mother—a china cabinet with large glass panels in the front. It was filled with beautiful china and other exquisite dishes.

As we chatted about Africa, she revealed extensive knowledge about African culture, and more importantly, she had a great deal of respect for its people. Yet, there was a humility about her that I liked. When she told me her mother had never allowed anyone on the movie set to compliment her, as a child, I understood why she never got impressed about being a star. It made her easy to talk to.

As our crew finished setting up the cameras, and we were about to start the interview, we heard a yell, and looking around we saw the huge arc lights headed for the glass front of the china cabinet. Everything would be broken to bits, but somehow, the heavy frame hit the edge of the cabinet, just missing the glass panels by inches, and chipped off a piece of wood before it crashed to the floor.

The Ambassador remained calm through it all. She looked at the huge mess on the floor and said, "I'm sure that can be cleaned up in no time. Let's get on with the interview." I liked Shirley Temple Black.

SHIRLEY MacLAINE

Another pleasant surprise came from Shirley MacLaine. This show came near the end of my three years at KQED, where the politics had gotten heavy as well. I felt my voting record on the board was in conflict with the show. Our attempt to keep *Newsroom* on the air along with other matters, kept me in hot water at the station.

I was no longer allowed to ask my own questions. This stab at my credibility just rolled off my back. I took the questions, typed on little cards, and went over them. I was also told not to bring up the subject of Shirley's long-distance relationship with her husband, Steve Parker, who lived in Japan.

The interview was to take place in Shirley's plush apartment in New York. I went to New York and we had a camera crew out of the PBS station there. I had read her latest book on China, describing the trip she took with ten American women from very diverse backgrounds and observing their reactions.

When Shirley entered the room, you knew you were in the presence of a star. She hardly wore any makeup, and seemed to have an inner glow. She looked soft, young and innocent. In a business that demands that you become tough as nails to survive, how she managed that, I'll never know.

We chatted a bit as the crew set up, and we struck a rapport.

She was seated on a long couch facing me, smiling. I sat at the end of the couch facing her. The interview began. I asked her how she got her start in show business, sticking closely to the questions on the cards.

"What was that?" she asked.

I repeated the question. She looked exasperated. "What else have you got there?" she asked. I started saying something about Carol Haney breaking her leg on Broadway, which gave her a chance to play the lead role, launching her to instant stardom. That did it! She leaned forward, gently took the cards from my hand, threw them on the couch behind her, leaned back and softly said, "Now let's have a real interview."

The cameras had caught it all!

I immediately launched into her trip to China. "Shirley, you recently took a very diverse group of American women to China. What were their reactions to the people there?" She told about the women she had picked and how the impact of China's culture challenged long held ideologies of everyone on the trip.

The treatment of the children had particularly fascinated them, and some refused to believe what they saw: very happy Chinese children—alert, beautiful and bright, in a communist country.

Somewhere along the line, she began talking about her own daughter, then offered: "She has a great relationship with me and with her father, Steve Parker." Everyone stood perfectly still. The subject had been broached, and by Shirley herself, so I felt safe in pursuing it. We talked about her unorthodox marriage and her unique relationship with her husband.

When the interview was over, she stood up and she hugged me warmly. I thanked her for a great interview.

Back in San Francisco, I had hoped they would leave the card snatching episode in because it was so impromptu, and gave insight into the real Shirley MacClaine, which is what television should be all about. The producers decided to edit it out because, they said, it made me look bad on camera. Funny, I thought it made the show!

Before *Turnabout* left the air in 1979, I interviewed two more great ladies: Toni Morrison, and Maya Angelou.

TONI MORRISON

Toni Morrison had just written her third book, *Song of Solomon*, published in 1977, when she arrived for an interview at **KQED**. The book had launched her into the rare atmosphere of storytelling genius that made her an instant icon. The first two, **The Bluest Eye,** followed by **Sula,** published in 1973. **Tar Baby**, was published in 1981, and was followed by **Beloved**, in 1987, which won her the Pulitzer Prize for Literature in 1988, and later made into a movie starring Oprah Winfrey.

Her books all succeed in opening up the Black psyche in new ways. Her search for love and identity pioneered a new generation of Black women writers who explore the African-American experience and relationships between men and women, friendship between women, and Black and White issues. Her metaphors are so deep they relate to people everywhere. Toni weaves a magic spell with words. She recounted how she had been raised by a family of storytellers, who kept alive stories about Africa and the roots that would one day make her a great author. After discussing her books, we talked about the Black family. She had raised two boys as a single mother, and I had raised three. We talked about the hazards of raising boys alone in an urban environment, something we had in common.

Song of Solomon won her the National Book Award and secured her appointment to the American Academy of Arts & Letters and the National Council of the Arts. We discussed the themes of her books and the powerful impact of literature on society.

Toni Morrison has conquered great odds to raise her sons, succeeded in the publishing world at Random House and now has become a very famous writer who later would receive the Nobel Prize in Literature. She is currently a Professor at Princeton.

I realized that I was in the presence of an icon, a woman who had reached down deep into a spiritual place to make us all explore the grand possibilities of who we really are as human beings. Her monumental contribution to African-American literature has made her one of the most celebrated writers of our time.

MAYA ANGELOU

I first met Maya Angelou back in the 1950's, when she was singing at the Purple Onion nightclub. She was tall and elegant. My brother, Stan Wilson, who was singing folk songs across the street at the famous **Hungri I** introduced us.

She was about to begin a national show for PBS, out of the studios of KQED, called *Blacks, Blues, Black*. In our interview, Maya talked about her long journey as a Professional Dancer and her 1954 tour of Europe and Africa in *Porgy and Bess*. That trip changed her life. She spent five years in Egypt and Ghana, where she worked as a journalist and University Professor. She was very close to Malcolm X and was active during the Civil Rights Movement.

Her most impressive talent, however, turned out to be writing. This was actually my third interview with her. In 1977, we flew down to her home in Pacific Palisades to do it. She had just finished writing *Sisters, Sisters,* a television show for one of the networks, and was quite thrilled about it. Little did she expect the ensuing battle and the years it would take to get that show finally on the air. In the interview she also talked about the difficulty of getting positive Black stories televised, problems in the publishing industry, as well as all the progress that had been made. Maya Angelou has done much to inspire young Black poets. Her poem *And Still I Rise,* is one of the most popular poems of our time.

Maya has had a varied career, as a Dancer, Poet and a distinguished career in television. Her first book of poetry, *Just and Give me a Cool Drink of Water, 'Fore I Die,* published in 1971, was nominated for a Pulitzer Prize. The first volume of her autobiography, *I Know Why The Caged Bird Sings,* was published in 1970, and became a best seller, and was followed by four other volumes. In 1993 she published a collection of essays, *Wouldn't Take Nothing For My Journey Now* and *On the Pulse of Morning,* which she was honored to read at President Clinton's 1983 Inauguration.

Maya Angelou has struck at the heart of aspiring young writers and poets of all races, creeds and colors, which has won her admiration and respect all over the world. Her personal journey has been one of struggle and perseverance, and has made her a very special woman of her time.

During these interviews in the late 1970's, these two women were rising stars and talked about the pitfalls and rewards of the publishing business. Black authors during the 1950's, 60's and 70's were scarce and Black women authors even more so. The strides Black writers have made in the publishing world can be directly attributed to the pioneers of that time: Lorraine Hansberry, James Baldwin, Ralph Ellison, Ishmael Reed, Gwendolyn Brooks, Alice Walker, Toni Morrison and Maya Angelou, along with those who preceded and came after them.

*   *   *

I should not leave the world of television without covering some of the techniques that are used to make this industry what it is. Television is magic, and has the power to inform, enchant, enrich, teach and dazzle. It also has the power to deceive, falsify, demean, stereotype, divide and conquer. When and how these techniques are used often vary. It is the public's responsibility to see to it that this medium is used for the benefit of Humankind and to improve the quality of life.

The camera is a powerful tool. It brings us images of beauty, grandeur, poverty, wealth, riots, crime, propaganda and news. It invades our living rooms every day of our lives. It is the new storyteller, and it tells the story exactly the way it wants to.

Everything depends on lights. Stories of photographer Ansel Adams waiting hours for just the right light are not exaggerated. It tells you the difference lighting makes in photographs, in your living space, on our streets, in our buildings and cities. In television and movies, lighting can make or break you. When a person is not properly lit, they appear unpleasing to the eye. The Kennedy/Nixon debates have often been cited as a classic case. Kennedy had the right lighting, make-up and haircut. Nixon had little makeup, an ill-fitting shirt collar, and in close-ups, appeared to sweat. Nixon was sabotaged by camera and lighting and Kennedy won the election.

Camera shots can be used to photograph your best side, or your worst. You can tell an upcoming star by how many close-ups he or she may get. If an actor doesn't get a close-up, the audience doesn't really get to know him. You get attached to a face up close. It's intimate. In Nixon's case it was used against him.

Many a story can change between the interview and actual airing.

Once the interview is done, the person interviewed may leave, while the reporter re-states the questions facing the camera. How the questions are asked, editing of the story, voice over, all contribute to how that story will look on the air.

One of the most important parts of a scene or interview is what is lurking in the background. It tells who you are. Most scholars, doctors, lawyers and scientists, have books behind them during an interview. Women of beauty and culture have an array of beautiful flowers in a lovely vase as background. Politicians usually have an American flag. You are not looking at it directly, but subconsciously; how you feel about people is connected to what is directly behind them. Always notice your surroundings when you are doing a television interview.

All of these things can be used for or against a person, depending on who is telling the story. You have to be aware of how you are being portrayed on camera.

In newspapers, it is location—where a story appears and what stories appear next to and around it. If a news story appears on the Obituary Page—well, you get the idea. It is another game and the insiders read it like a book. You can tell who is in and who is out just by whether or not their names appear in the newspaper, and what is said about them when the names do appear. If they are not mentioned at all, they are definitely out. There are plenty of names on that blacklist!

It pays to pay attention to media and how it slants, stereotypes, omits and manages news through its use of these techniques. It creates its own environment that results in how we are all perceived. First Amendment rights should extend to all, not just to those who own the media.

As I discovered these subtle ways the media can slant and distort, I tried to circumvent it whenever possible. For instance, in the 70's, lighting was not as kind to Black skin as it is today. I often advised people of color to wear clothing that would enhance their projection on the screen. I also asked the lighting people to remember that black skin soaked up light and needed more lighting than guests with white skin.

Today's television technology has advanced on all levels, and now one can only hope we can do as well with content.

Jerri Lange

*   *   *

In 1979, I had reached an impasse in my career in broadcasting in San Francisco. After serving on the **KQED** board for three years, I resigned. My show, "**Turnabout**" left the air and I decided to make a change. The television industry had closed its doors to me and I was "blackballed" in my efforts to work again in the Bay Area. I published a magazine, continued to teach at San Francisco State University, and became a media consultant.

CHAPTER VI

WORLD TRAVELER

One learns so much from travel. Meeting the people of each country is a rewarding experience that leaves you with a better understanding of their cultures. What it also does is reveal much about life and our role as women. Whenever I teach a class I tell my students "forget about buying that car—travel instead." As women, we have allowed ourselves to be locked into one culture with one point of view, in a world rich in diversity. The only way to understand the world is to visit it. Being up close and personal with people different than you will enrich your life beyond measure. You will get in touch with yourself as never before, and learn what it is to be an international woman. As a Broadcaster in a changing environment, it is imperative that we try to understand the world we are reporting.

The people of South America have a resilience and love of life, in the midst of poverty, that is hard to explain. They seem to be happier than their North American counterparts-Black or White. They are less uptight and more accepting of others. Since my travels in the 1970s, I am sure the drug trade and internal conflicts that plague those countries have taken their toll on the people. But when I think of Brazil, I still think of the Samba.

Sweden was one of the most beautiful countries I have ever seen. Clean air and water, healthy food and drink, and warm and friendly people, are all in abundance. The perplexing social problems facing the Swedes is still a paradox. The lovely Royal Wedding of King Gustav XVI, remains a high point of my travels in Europe. London and Paris still have the excitement and history that captures the imagination. For me, those two cities would be easiest to live in abroad. There is so much culture to explore, it would probably take a lifetime.

Africa was both exciting and troubling to me. I was moved spiritually to return to my homeland, but troubled to see so much tribal warfare still going on. The iron grip of colonialism was also present in so many subtle ways. Even so, Africans have an unmistakable nobility that comes with the territory. They must be seen on their own turf, engaged in their ancient rituals to truly be appreciated. I hope in their pursuit of Western culture and ideas, they never lose their cultural richness and strong spirit that has carried them this far and made them the oldest living people on earth.

SOUTH AMERICA

In 1975, during a conference for the International Year of the Woman, I was invited by members of the American Women For International Understanding to accompany them on a State Department-sponsored tour of five South American countries: Colombia, Argentina, Brazil, Chile and Peru. I was the only African American woman on the trip. These women were from all walks of life: a doctor from Los Angeles, a judge from San Francisco, two editors—one from the **San Francisco Chronicle**, the other from the **Examiner**. Several writers were also in the group, and Florence Eldridge March, widow of actor Frederic March. I represented the Media.

We would meet the top professional and working class women in each country and exchange ideas. I had just finished wrapping up as moderator for the conference that had taken place at a major downtown San Francisco hotel, where we had met with women from all over the world in a very candid exchange of ideas. Anti-American feeling was just beginning to spread throughout South America and this was to be a goodwill trip.

After making arrangements for shots and passports, ten women of various professions took off for South America. Our first stop was

Bogota, Colombia. As I recall, there was a curfew and things were very quiet in the streets that first night. All of South America was in turmoil at that time, as we would soon find out.

One of the highlights of the trip was meeting the women and talking to them about their professions and raising their families. We visited many interesting places, but the one that stands out is the Gold Museum. I remember being surrounded by little third or fourth grade children who seemed to be wondering what nationality I was. The people of Columbia were of Spanish and Indian ancestry. They saw very few Black people, since the only South American country that engaged in slave trade was Brazil. They had never seen a Black American woman before. As the group of children continued asking questions, interpreted by their teacher, I told them of my various bloodlines; when I pulled off my hat and they saw my "natural" hairstyle, they cried out, almost in unison, "Africana, muy bonita!" They, too, thought Black was beautiful and expressed it in such a loving way. They followed me all around the Museum for the rest of the tour.

On the way to Buenos Aires, Argentina, we stopped at a beautiful place called Iguassu Falls. It is on the border between Argentina and Brazil. It is known for its pink falls, an effect caused by the rich, red soil of Argentina. We waved to people standing across the water in Brazil. The hotel we stopped at was also pink, and we were greeted with a glass of pink champagne. No wonder it is a popular destination for honeymooners! The old wooden bridge was rickety but strong, and led directly to the Falls. The showers were so heavy that you were given a raincoat to wear. At certain times of day, rainbows glittered because of the mixture of sun and water, and I suddenly found myself standing in the center of a rainbow! It was a sight to behold. That scene would set the stage for my most surprising encounter. I was about to experience culture shock.

While I was in the middle of the bridge, I looked back at the hotel and saw a very tall Black man, with a small Japanese older woman. I couldn't hear what they were saying as they were quite a distance away. As the man started toward me, I begin to see him more clearly. He had a large, soft "natural", and distinct Japanese features. He was a Black

Japanese, child of a World War II Black soldier and a Japanese woman. Many of these Black Japanese people had come to live in Sao Paolo because they were considered "gaijin" or outsiders, people of non-Japanese descent. The Japanese took good care of them, and they worked in the Toyota automobile industry in Sao Paolo. I later found out that the second largest population of Japanese in the world is in Sao Paolo.

As he came toward me he stared at me as hard as I was staring at him; with the showers drenching us from the waterfall, rainbows surrounding us, I had the strangest feeling of two ships passing in the night, ripped from their African homeland, transported overseas to another country and distant culture. We were far apart, yet so close together in a moment of time. It is an experience I shall never forget.

When we got to Buenos Aires, things changed. We arrived late at the Plaza Hotel and were informed that our rooms were gone. Florence Eldridge March, on her first trip since the death of her husband, wasn't buying any of it. We all had a meeting in the ladies rest room of the hotel. We decided to stage a sit-in the ladies room of the hotel. Florence took her place on one of the lounges, some of us took available chairs, and the others took to the floor. We would not budge until they restored our rooms. By the time the State Department heard of it, things had begun to move. We not only got our rooms back, but large baskets of fruit and a bottle of wine arrived at our rooms. Hotels at that time were booked solid and rooms were at a premium, so we concluded that any late arrivals were not given a grace period. We were lucky.

When we got to Santiago, Chile, it was just after the military coup by General Augusto Pinochet against President Salvador Allende and anti-American feelings were running high. Soldiers armed with machine guns escorted us to a meeting that had been arranged with the wife of General Pinochet. It was her first interview with an American delegation. We passed the Presidential Palace. It still had bullet holes in the walls from the violent takeover of Allende's government. When we arrived for the interview with Mme. Pinochet, our passports were confiscated, and we were escorted by machine guns up to an office in one of the large government buildings. We were told we could not ask questions about the coup, only about the family and other non-political subjects. Mme. Pinochet looked like any other wife, mother, or grandmother, as she talked about her children and family. She seemed not to be a part of it all. People were taking our pictures the whole time we were there. We were later told that we were the first Americans to visit since the coup, and every precaution was being taken to avoid an international incident. The politically charged atmosphere required additional security measures. In case anything happened during the interview, our photographs would be plastered all over the country! After the interview our passports were returned. All I can really remember vividly about the whole event are the machine guns.

What I remember most about Rio de Janeiro is the music. It was everywhere. The poor people lived in the mountains and the wealthy resided in the lowlands—the reverse of the custom in North America. I was told that when the heavy rains came it washed the cardboard houses down the mountain, children and all. The people ran down the mountain, picked up their corrugated tin roofs and furniture and would samba back up the hill. They were a very resilient people. Further, I sensed a kind of joy that was missing in Blacks from North America. I would later find that it was because the slaves who landed in Brazil were allowed to keep their language, religion, and much of their culture. The result is "Macumba," a combination of Catholic and African religion. Bahia was the first capital of Brazil, and African culture flourished during that time. This led to the wonderful rhythms that came out of South America, and all the exciting Latin dances that are now sweeping the world. The people also created "Carnaval." *NHK*, the Japan Broadcasting Station, has done a definitive documentary on the grassroots beginnings of Carnaval and how it has evolved to its current status and importance in Rio de Janeiro.

We visited Copacabana Beach. In the evenings I would hear a kind of thunder near sunset. It was Brazilians rushing to the beach to see the sunset! We also stopped at Ipanema, the beach where the famous song "*Girl From Ipanema*" was written. It is a true story. The girl who was just fourteen years old is now grown and married, and the lovesick older man who wrote the song is still there too. The locals love to re-tell the story. I ended up playing soccer with some very youthful Brazilian boys on the beach.

Cuzco, Peru was 11,000 feet elevation and I had a headache the whole four days I was there. We were given coca tea and told to rest and take it easy. We were to walk very slowly, as we tried to get our breath. Once we felt better, we were off to Macchu Pichu, a mountaintop Inca city that was dug up and restored. We took a four hour train ride to the mountains, and as we reached even higher ground, we finally entered the grounds of the city. It is so special, one has to make the visit to understand it. There is something spiritual there, and the buildings are ancient and still intact. We saw the granaries, the prison, small houses, a place where ancient people lived. On the way up we stopped to photograph picturesque women in tall hats and warm clothing. They were tending the flocks of llamas on the mountainsides, and had their children with them. When we got up close, we found out they were stoned, from chewing coca leaves to keep warm. We also found a wonderful stream of water, where we bathed our faces. The stream was clear as crystal and from an unknown source. It was said to have mystical powers.

The flight out of Peru would have made a terrific movie. The airline told us we had to wait for a certain wind velocity or the plane would crash into the Andes mountains which surround Cuzco. We all waited with our on board baggage in the airport, waiting for the winds to pick up. We were told to watch the pilot of the plane. When he made a dash for the plane we were to follow. After three hours of waiting, the pilot started his dash toward the plane, with the rest of us in hot pursuit. We scrambled aboard the plane, strapped ourselves in, and prayed as the airplane took off. When we made it over the beautiful Andes mountains, we all cheered. It was a very scary experience—one I hope never to go through again.

SWEDEN

In 1976, I was invited by the Swedish Consulate to attend the annual Nordic Screening, an eleven-day event, which took place in Stockholm. Each year five Scandinavian countries showcase their new television programs for International distribution: Sweden, Norway, Denmark, Iceland and Finland were the participating countries. I would be attending from the West Coast and several people would come from the East Coast. The group included: Candy Martin from the Corporation for Public Broadcasting; Peggy Charren, founder and President of Action for Children's Television and Nicholas Johnson, former member of the Federal Communications Commission, who currently headed an independent broadcasting monitoring organization. In addition, there were two executives from PBS. Nick Johnson and I were friends from the first time I had interviewed him in the early 70s at **KBHK**. A powerful, dissenting voice on the **FCC,** Nick could not be compromised.

My first night in Stockholm, before I met up with my American companions, was an experience in itself. I arrived on a rainy Sunday night. I was very hungry after the long trip. Everything was closed. I walked the wet, rainy streets until I found a small restaurant that was open. No one in the restaurant spoke English. I sat and struggled with the menu, when suddenly a young Swedish man headed in my direction. He introduced himself (I shall call him Jon), and then sat down and asked in perfect English if I was having trouble ordering dinner. He asked what I liked, and he ordered a lovely delicate white fish called "Cos", served in a creamy white sauce. It was the sweetest white fish I have ever tasted. He ordered a salad, wine and dessert. He then asked me where I was from. When I replied San Francisco, he told me he had just come back from there and what a coincidence to run into me. He was only 19 years old. Jon asked if I would like to meet some of his friends and go discoing at the Alexandra, a famous disco where young King Gustav XVI used to dance, before his engagement. His marriage was to take place the following week. I accepted.

The next night it was off to Alexandra's. The first thing I noticed was the music. They were not playing Swedish music, but Black music! Muddy Waters, and the low-down, gut bucket, funky blues, from way, way down South. Jazz and the Blues are loved all over the world. It took a long time for Jazz to find a niche in American culture. Along with Country Music, it was America's cultural stepchild. They have both, finally, been given their rightful place. The Swedes had no such hangup, and were free to enjoy the music in its pure essence. And enjoy it, they did!

We jammed and danced the night away. When we stepped outside, it was two in the morning and still daylight. A strange dusk lit the sky. We were in the middle of Sweden's summer, the Land of the Midnight Sun. When it should be dark, it was daylight. Night never comes. It can be strange and unnerving. In one sense the sun never sets. This lasts for six months. When the reverse happens, there is darkness for six months. This can be very depressing, so many Swedes head for Spain and other Mediterranean countries for the sun.

One morning, while listening to Swedish Radio, I was surprised to hear classical music played on the same program with Black music and other forms of music, probably because they have fewer radio stations than in the United States. When the announcer suddenly broke into English to announce, "We will now hear "I'll Be Glad When You're Dead, You Rascal You," by Louis Armstrong," I knew I was going to love this country.

When Jon took me to a concert in the park, located in the middle of the city, I thought I knew what to expect. What I did not expect to hear were Swedish musicians playing and a girl singer racing up and down the stage shouting, "Rollin', rollin', rollin' down the river." The girl moved just like Tina Turner. By the time we hit another local jazz club, *Stampen*, I realized that the Swedes love Black music. Black tourists in the '70s were so rare in Sweden that when the Swedish musicians played a particular note, they discreetly looked over at me. When I nodded my head in agreement, they would burst into smiles. They were playing for me!

Jon was helping me change my view of Sweden as a blonde, blue-eyed mecca, filled with classical music floating through the air. These people understood pain and they felt it in the music of Black people: Muddy Waters and the Blues. They experienced it deep down inside their soul. I would soon find out just how deeply they felt, when I stumbled upon the other side of this beautiful country. Sweden was not all paradise. In spite of one of the very highest standards of living in the world—Sweden was plagued by drug addiction, alcoholism and one of the highest suicide rates in the world. This was particularly true among the youth. Jon later confided to me he had been writing a suicide note in the restaurant the night we met. They were bored to death, they said, because everything was handed to them. Dropouts in school were on the increase, and in one instance, I saw a gang, dressed in black leather jackets, harassing motorists out of their cars.

I tried to find some answers. Upon reflection I found I was moving among a deep, reflective people, who were very aware of the pain and injustices all over the world. They were often called to different countries as Peace Keepers. Sweden was a neutral country that—in modern times—had never been to war. It was allowed into countries that were off-limits to many others, especially those at war. I surmised the Vikings had settled their role as warriors centuries ago, and had nothing more to prove. I arranged a meeting between Jon and Nick Johnson to give Nick an interview for his radio show which was broadcast to more than 140 stations in the United States. Nick explored some of the problems in depth and got a great interview.

By now, I was consulting with the Establishment by day, and running with Jon and his young friends by night. I saw two sides of this lovely country. I began asking questions of my daytime hosts, questions that had emerged from my midnight excursions with the young Swedes. At first, they were a little reluctant to talk, but when they saw that my interest went far beyond criticism, that I was truly searching for understanding, they opened up. I began to notice that as soon as I broached a question on a certain subject, the next day would find me seated next to the person who was an expert in that particular field.

One Sunday, I was invited to dinner with a woman who was the Director of the Elementary Schools. She frankly told me that many of the children were hyperactive. I told her that we had done studies in the United States, showing poor diet was largely responsible for such behavior, but that malnutrition could hardly be a factor in Sweden. She agreed, and said they were still looking for answers. I told her about the contrast I had just seen the year before in South America.

In Brazil, poor people lived in houses that rolled down the hill during a good rain. The family picked up the pieces and not only kept right on living, but sang songs about it! What is there about human nature that clings to and reveres life under the worst of conditions, then tries to throw it away when it has everything? Are we born to deal only with conflict? Is Humankind unprepared to deal with real happiness? Maybe there is guilt when one country has so much, while others starve. Were the teenagers of Sweden sensitive to this? Neither of us had the answer to those questions.

I suggested that perhaps we could one day invite the people of Brazil to participate in a seminar with the technological countries, perhaps in Sweden, for an exchange of ideas, and perhaps explore some of these complex issues.

Candy Martin, from CPB, and I were asked whether we would like to cover the upcoming wedding of King Gustav XVI. We jumped at the chance. It was a courtesy extended to us, making us a part of the accredited journalists, 1200 in all, who would be coming from all over the world. When we picked up our credentials, we were asked what language we preferred. The press kits were printed in four languages and told you everything you ever wanted to know about a Royal Wedding. The information came in a handsome, black leather case, and contained a complete list of all Royalty attending, backgrounds on the Royal couple, our assignment slot, press passes, the map covering the processional route through the streets of Stockholm after the wedding, along with all the celebrations for the event. It was a rare time to be in Sweden. It had been many years since there had been a Royal Wedding in Europe. All royal guests stayed at the Grand Hotel.

Very few journalists could get near the church on the day of the wedding, because it was crowded with Royalty from all over the world. I accepted an invitation to watch the whole thing on television. A producer from Swedish Radio invited a Dutch journalist and me to watch the proceedings at his home in the country. While in this home-like setting, I paused to remember, that I had only met one Black person during this entire trip—an Opera singer from the United States, who was married to a Swedish businessman. Yet I never felt out of place or patronized in any way.

Imagine if you can, what a city is like when one hundred and eight broadcasters from all over the world, join 1200 members of the international press, to meet at the same time for a Royal Wedding.

The royal couple rode in a beautiful horse-drawn carriage through the streets, thronged with thousands of cheering Swedes. Ships in the harbor shot cannon-like salutes, with whistles blowing and huge sprays of water bursting from the sides of vessels like fountains gone mad!

One of the loveliest events ending our Conference was a ride up the graceful waterways that surround Stockholm. Once through the Archipelagos, there stands another Grand Hotel, carefully hidden. In the middle of a small forest stood this rare jewel displaying the ultimate in European luxury. I sat down to a dinner fit for a Queen.

One last evening before my departure, Nick Johnson and I were invited to a lovely dinner in the countryside of Sweden. Almost every Swedish family has a home in the countryside. This one was on the water, and it was mandatory to take a boat ride before dinner. One of the guests, I was told, was the 'Walter Cronkite' of Sweden. We had deep discussions about our experiences, as Americans, in their country. One of my questions was about the young people. I asked: "What could a Swedish youth, with a needle in his arm, have in common, with a Black youth in Harlem, with a needle in his arm?" No one had an answer, and as we have now come to know, it is a question being asked in affluent homes all over the world. Before I checked out of my hotel back in Stockholm, I got a call from the United States Embassy asking if there was anything they could do to make my trip home a pleasant one. I told them I would be stopping off in London and Paris before returning home. The call was comforting, as if there had been an invisible friend available had I needed one. It made me feel safe away from home and instilled a feeling of pride in my country and the joy of being an American abroad without the ugly specter of racism to spoil it all.

PARIS

It had been almost six years since my first trip to Paris in 1970, and I could hardly wait to walk the Champs Elysees once again. The French have a way of presenting food in its proper environment. Breads are baked fresh each day, and come in every imaginable shape. There may be croissants baked around the world, but they do not taste like the ones in Paris. The vegetables and cheeses are all fresh and a combination of all of these aromas, once inhaled, will make you a gourmet critic forever.

I was able to find a darling little hotel. It had no elevator and I had to walk up three flights, but the cost of the room included breakfast, served in my room each morning by a handsome young man. It was all so civilized! It was located just over a bakery, and each morning I was awakened by the smell of French croissants being baked at dawn. I thought I was in heaven.

Paris is a walking town. I tried in vain to turn a corner on a square block like we do in the United States, but the streets of Paris are laid out diagonally, and the result is startling. When you turn a corner in Paris the architecture jumps out at you, and almost knocks you down. In a way you are kissed—Paris style. No wonder they call it the City of Love.

Everything about it is romantic: the way the sun hits the streets, the way it lights up at night, the incredible food, and most of all, the way couples stroll down the street, oblivious of everyone. It is a magical city.

I flew from Paris to London, where I stayed a few days, and on the Fourth of July was able to get a plane home. I arrived home in San Francisco at about nine in the evening, just in time for the fireworks. I put my suitcases down, grabbed an elevator to the roof of my apartment building, and saw a magnificent display of fireworks. It felt like a welcome home.

*   *   *

AFRICA

After I resigned from the Board of *KQED* in 1979, I was invited to take a Pan Am Inaugural flight along with others to Africa. I had been chosen because of my battles on the Board of *KQED* and my struggles with the television industry to make it more sensitive to minorities. We could visit any country we wished as guests of Pan Am, paying only for hotel and other expenses. The only stipulation was that we must be in Nairobi, Kenya for Jomo Kenyatta Day, honoring the former

President of Kenya. I was filled with joy and anticipation at finally visiting the home of my ancestors. Other invited guests from the West Coast were two friends of mine, Naomi Gray and Effie Lee Morris.

Our first stop was Dakar, Senegal. The first thing you notice is the electricity in the air. Africans are a people of high energy. They are alive! The other thing you notice is the colors. People wear bright colors. Against black skin it is something to behold. Everyone seemed to wear gold. It was the number one ornament. The women are stunning. Many of them are mixed with tribes from the Sudan, their neighboring country, and the women braid their hair, with ribbons interwoven to match whatever dress they are wearing. They were wearing the braided hairstyles back in the '70's, that would soon catch on in the United States with African American women. (Bo Derek made it her beauty mark in the movie "*10*"). African women ran the hotels, and dressed in flowing, feminine attire. They also handled the business and finances. The men functioned as head of the family, were active in politics and supported their wives in business.

We stayed at a French hotel and ate dinner on the lawns of the restaurant. That evening we were treated to a beautiful performance by *Les Ballets Africains*. The waiters were happy to greet us and began to tell us what tribes we were descended from. We asked how they could do that since we had so many racial mixtures. They said that African blood was so strong that the forehead, eyes and bridge of the nose never changed. You always carried the mark of your tribe. He said I was descended from a Yoruba Nomadic tribe. The most startling thing about Africa is to see Africans in most of the jobs. Not only waiters, but hotel executives, store owners, even African pilots and stewardesses in control of the airplanes.

The next evening we had dinner on board a boat, complete with all the ambiance of a French restaurant. The waiter brought our lobsters over to us while still alive, then brought them back perfectly prepared. We drank Mateus wine, and I realized I had never been aware of this side of Africa before. The architecture is a holdover from the colonial French, and I felt just like I was in Sausalito! There is a large French population in Dakar, which projects a subtle colonial presence still conducting business in Africa. A great deal of European business goes on all over Africa, particularly with mining companies, hotels, and other kinds of business related to trade, especially those that involve exporting Africa's vast natural resources. It is the control of these contracts for mineral wealth that is at the heart of the problems in Africa today.

The most memorable trip was to the Isle of Goree, where the slave ships took off for the Americas—North and South. We had a young boy of about 11 years of age as our guide. He was fluent in four languages: English, French, Wolof (his native language) and another tribal language. He apologized for his English, but we reminded him we did not speak his language, and that he was multilingual in four languages! He knew the entire history of Goree and was a warm and gracious host. He was dressed in old clothes, but he said he was studying to become a doctor; he hoped to continue his studies abroad and come back and help his people. Effie Lee visited the schools and said the children only had pencils and notebooks, but were studying science, math and languages. They had none of the modern conveniences or materials of American schools. They were told they had to study and become doctors, lawyers, engineers, and return to help their country. I thought back to my counselor at Berkeley High School who told me "there is nothing for your people in this country," while advising me to study for a service occupation rather than enter the University of California. (At age 36, I would go back to Merritt College and score 98.2 in the entrance exam, and later become a Broadcast journalist, writer and college professor). African children may not have the modern materials that can be found in most classrooms in the United States, but they have what counts most: dedicated teachers and motivated students.

We visited the old building where our ancestors left for the Americas. Some of the slaves went to South America, so maybe I passed some of my relatives when I was in Brazil. There was a door marked Door of No Return: Slaves either boarded the ship, dove into the ocean and drowned, or were shot if they tried to go back. But no one returned through that door. I brought back dirt from the floor of the room marked Recalcitrant Slaves. I am sure that's where my ancestors came from.

J e r r i

Arriving in Nairobi for Jomo Kenyatta Day was next on our itinerary. It was the festive occasion when Kenyans celebrated the life of Jomo Kenyatta, who brought about their liberation. His tomb is lit with the eternal flame and sits near a lovely park. Naomi, Effie Lee and I stayed at the Hotel Stanley, where people checked in from all over the world. Naomi visited local businesswomen and tried to arrange exports of their beautiful handwoven fabrics.

An African couple invited me to visit what they called refugee camps, which were off limits to visitors. They said they would escort me. After a ride into the country, I begin to see the shacks that had been set up. The poverty was unbelievable. These were the Ugandans who had fled the reign of Idi Amin. There seemed to be thousands of people living out in the open with small temporary shelters set up.

I later visited the U.S. Embassy at a lunch given by Swedish Ambassador Cecelia Nettlebrant, whom I had met in San Francisco when she was assigned there. I spoke of the vast contrasts of life in Africa—between the rich and poor. I met Dr. Yusuf Ali Eraj, a Muslim Pakistani doctor, whose family had been in Nairobi for four generations. He owned a clinic in the heart of Nairobi. He offered to take me to an African village, where I later saw many children who, according to Dr. Eraj, would not live long, because of their diet. It lacked protein, which was the basic food needed to survive. He showed me a fifty year-old woman, who was wrinkled, walked with a cane and looked like she was eighty years old. She had lived a long life in comparison to the others. When I told him I was fifty-six years old, he was shocked. He later invited me to his home for dinner. One of his sons was also a doctor, and he asked if they could pinch my skin to show what a woman looks like when she receives the proper nutrition.

All of this was depressing to me, so it was uplifting to visit a Masai village. The Masai are a special people. Fierce warriors, they are revered as hunters, respected for their intelligence, skill and beauty. Their villages were clean and orderly. They make beautiful woodcarvings and sculpture. Their nobility is evident throughout the entire culture, and they are held in high esteem all over the Continent.

Despite the political upheavals caused by border closings and well-known tribal differences, Africans were getting together to solve their mutual problems, particularly concerning the environment. I met with a group of environmentalists from over ten countries, at the Kenyatta Conference Center, a magnificent building where most of the meetings were held. It seats 4,000 people. Africa had entered the 20th century and found itself plagued with some of the same problems of the developed nations around the world. Pollution in Africa was at an all time high and children from ages 2-4 were dying of lung disease. Tribes from all over Africa were represented. There are 48 tribes in Kenya; the largest and ruling tribe is the Kikuyu, with the Masai the second largest. I filed a story on Africa with the *San Francisco Chronicle*, about all the projects going on in Africa to meet the needs of technology. ***Black Africa, Facing Up To Its Growing Pains*** (Wed. Nov. 21, 1979), was published in the "Briefing" section of the paper after my return home.

Our last stop was Monrovia, Liberia. As soon as we hit the city we felt bad vibes. Hostility was thick. Revolution was in the air. We didn't recognize it at first. At the hotel the waiters were not friendly to us. Anti-American feelings were high.

Liberia has a rocky history. The United States sent in William V.S. Tubman and his family to rule the country. They were descendants of slaves and highly resented by the local tribes. They were not kind rulers and were often accused of corruption. William P. Tolbert, Jr., was the current President of the country. We stayed a couple of uncomfortable days, and after hearing that an uprising was imminent, we decided to leave immediately. Some months later, in 1980, we read of the murders of the ruling family and others who were in Monrovia at the time. We shuddered, and felt that we got out just in time.

Much has changed in Africa since that trip back in 1979. AIDS has become the overriding problem in that vast continent, and the struggle for survival is even more crucial. My visit completed a circle, by taking me back to my ancestors. It also served to remind me of the deliberate, mean-spirited, destructive history of slavery. The courageous efforts of all those demanding reparations for the untold emotional, financial and spiritual damage to the descendants of those slaves is finally being recognized by the U.S. government as they look into the possibility of finally paying back for years of unpaid labor.

CHAPTER VII

MASTER CLASS

I first met Horace Cayton in 1964, while I was still at *The Chronicle*. He was one of the scheduled speakers on a show called *"Cities and Negroes,"* a three-unit Sunrise Semester course for San Francisco State University, taped at *KPIX*. I was one of the students chosen from our class to question a series of guest speakers on current issues. Horace Cayton was an African American Sociologist from Chicago.

My article on the Black family had appeared in the *San Francisco Chronicle* that Sunday. My teacher arranged for me to meet Cayton before our class.

He picked Cayton up at UC Berkeley where he was a visiting Professor in the Department of Sociology, and then picked me up on the way to the studio. When Cayton got out of the car to greet me, I said "I am a great admirer of yours, Mr. Cayton, and I have read your column regularly in the *Pittsburgh Courier.*" He looked at me and said, "You're not so bad yourself. I just read your article in the Sunday Section of *The Chronicle* on the Black family and it is very good." He had actually read something of mine.

I subsequently became his pupil. The knowledge he imparted to me during the next years would impact my career as a writer.

"Being a writer," he used to say, "has nothing to do at all with whether you get published. It has to do with how you view life. Some great writers are never published, and some people who publish are not writers at all. They are simply propagandists. A good writer observes life with a certain kind of detachment, while still being involved. "Just remember," he continued, "you are a writer. You wrote about how painful it is to be a Black woman in America and you wrote about it without bitterness or hostility. You simply lived it, observed it and wrote about it."

"Eugene O'Neill did the same thing," he said. "O'Neill observed the disintegration and pain in his family and wrote about it in *Long Day's Journey Into Night.* I remember being there on opening night on Broadway," he continued, "when the curtain came down, I couldn't move. I had to rush from the theatre and walk the streets of New York for hours. O'Neill had captured something of everyone's family: the failures, heartaches, the weaknesses, and most of all the pain that no one wants to talk about. He wrote about it, sparing no one, not even his own mother and father. He wrote about the family and what that means to each one of us."

Family had special meaning to Cayton because he had felt slighted at not being named after his famous grandfather, Hiram Rhodes Revels, the first African American Senator from the South, during the Reconstruction. A Methodist Minister and Educator, he was the son of former slaves. That honor had gone to his younger brother, Revels, whom he felt was his mother's favorite. He used to tell me how painful it was to write his autobiography *Long Old Road*; how he asked his mother, on her deathbed, whether or not he was her favorite, and how she had replied, "All I know, son, is that I'd like to die in peace." Horace said he could not read that passage in his book without crying, realizing that we are always concerned with our own pain, not the pain of others. "O'Neill captured this," he said, "and that's what hit me opening night of *Long Day's Journey Into Night.*"

I wanted to study with Cayton right away so that I could find out as much as possible about what makes a great writer, and engage in discussions of serious social problems of our time. I was pleased that he had an agenda, and that it was to pass on information that he had to give.

Cayton was anxious to tell me about his stay in Paris. He had gone there with several famous Black writers who were part of the *WPA*

(Works Progress Administration), Writer's Workshop that included such men as Langston Hughes, Arna Bontemps and Richard Wright. He was filled with anecdotes about everyone: how Nancy Cunard (of the Cunard Shipping Line) gave cocktail parties to meet all of the great writers of that day; how Paul Robeson attracted women; who the phonies were, who the real people were, and how to tell the difference.

Cayton was in constant trouble at U.C. Berkeley. They wanted him to be a Black sociologist, and he simply wanted to be a sociologist. They wanted him to study the ghetto. He and St. Clair Drake had already written two of the finest volumes on Black life in Chicago, *Black Metropolis*. He had studied with Dr. Robert Hutchins at the University of Chicago, and he and Drake had been commissioned to write a well-researched book on Black life at that time.

Cayton's work on *Black Metropolis*, written with St. Clair Drake, established him as one of the foremost scholars of Black history in America. It was a tremendous undertaking, as described by Cayton in his autobiography *Long Old Road*:

"We recruited our research assistants from the graduate students at the university. Throughout the life of the research—a period of about four years—approximately twenty research students in specialized fields participated in the collection and organization of material on various phases of Negro life. They were assisted by an office and field staff of approximately one hundred and fifty WPA workers, who acted as interviewers, clerks, typists, and statisticians. Tens of thousands of interviews were conducted with Negroes and whites from every walk of life; the files of Negro and white newspapers were researched, as were public documents of every type; census and statistical material was gathered from many sources; and the publications of the University of Chicago Press dealing with the city and the Negro community were studied and restudied. The project was perhaps the largest research effort ever concentrated on a single Negro community."

Perhaps Cayton's most telling interview came during a discussion with an African diplomat, back in the 1950's, as the first African American news reporter accredited to the United Nations. He worked for the *Pittsburgh Courier.* Cayton's question was, "What do you think of American Negroes now that you have met some of us?" The diplomat answered:

> "Frankly, I do not envy the position of the American Negro. Being a minority in a great White nation, you necessarily have goals and aspirations which I do not share and have difficulty understanding. Of course you wish to be free, to work and live like others. But you American Negroes have no separate culture, no traditions except those of slavery, and can have no ambitions except to be like other Americans. If you are successful, this will only lead to your eventual disappearance. You will become a part of the majority group. You are fighting, it seems to me, for your extinction—while we in Africa are fighting for a new civilization based upon our own culture and traditions. I would not know how to be an American Negro nor would I enjoy it. It is not that I believe the Black man is superior, although being a Black man I am proud of my race. But we have no ambition to be White. We as a people do not want to be swallowed up by the Whites, as must be your fate."

Much has changed since that interview. Black Americans have supported Africans in their fight for freedom throughout Africa, particularly in South Africa, where we stood side by side with Nelson Mandela in his fight for freedom. We have also kept alive our culture and heritage with music and art, and many African Americans can be seen at social events in braids, dreadlocks, and African attire.

What puzzled Cayton was that Black people never seemed to learn how to play the "political game." He talked about the two-party system being used by those without power, while the real decisions were made by a few elites at the top. The "game" never changed—only the decision over which party would rule. As I watched the recent Election

2000 presidential race, where even if you voted it did not count—I wondered what Cayton would have thought about that!

He believed that the problems of the ghetto had been studied to death, particularly in his two-part volume, and felt that racism would not be solved until somebody studied the problems in the White community, and he was the one to do it. No wonder he was in trouble. This idea would plant the seed for the three-part series I would later write and produce for **KEMO-TV**, entitled *"White Ghetto,"* which aired on September 2, 1968. I wrote that Webster's Dictionary states that a "ghetto is a part of a city in which members of a minority group live because of social, legal, or economic pressure." I felt that whites who choose to live together exclusively, in that kind of setting, qualify as a ghetto. A White announcer examined all the problems of that community and their impact on the community at large.

During Cayton's time at the University of California, he was a powerhouse of information. A confidential study had been done at UC, in the late 1950's, for instance, on the impact of technology on employment. Cayton said that by the 1980's machines and robots would be doing most of the work, and that by the 1990's only 20-30% of the work force would eventually be employed. The other 70%-80% would have to return to service occupations for the new elite—those who had jobs. The report was not made public because no one wanted to deal with the alternatives. With the dot com industry taking over most of the jobs and changing the nature of the job market, it is uncanny how far ahead sociologists can envision the future.

He said UC did another research study on how deep the establishment, through its behavioral scientists, reached into the bedrooms and sex habits of the population. Through intricate tracking systems, classes were kept divided, in the work place, in social settings, controlling future generations. You could move about all you wished, as long as you stayed in the area designed for you. I knew such a system had been put in place for Blacks, but was astonished to find out that one had been operating for Whites as well.

Perhaps most devastating was his revelation on how Black people in this country remain on a treadmill, carefully hidden, but expertly run by those in power. Horace Cayton would explain all of this and the reasons why unharnessed Black energy, like that displayed by Malcolm X, is so dangerous: it is unpredictable. It finally occurred to Cayton that he was getting nowhere with the University, and it began to get to him. He suffered because of desires and ambition and he turned to alcohol and drugs, LSD. It broke my heart to see this giant of a man going down, little by little.

Who could fathom a Horace Cayton? He was born in Seattle, Washington, son of a Republican newspaper publisher, tall, erect, with very large brown, almost dreamy eyes. He had very distinguished looking gray hair. He was heavy-set, a large man with a commanding air about him. When Horace entered a room he seemed to fill it with his presence. Where did he fit? A man who knew his grandfather was the first Senator from the South, during Black Reconstruction, Sen. Hiram Revels, who helped govern this country and shaped its policy during the post Civil War days; whose brother, Revels Cayton, helped turn the labor movement around in the 1930's.

I remember one evening we went out to dinner. Horace met me at the office, after an interview with the book editor, Bill Hogan. He had just written his autobiography, **Long Old Road**. Earlier, I had gone into Hogan's office and said, "Bill, I hope you give this review special treatment, because this man has laid his soul bare for all to see in this book."

He looked up and said, "Why don't you give me 400 words." That is how I came to write my first book review for the paper. Later that evening, we were celebrating publication of his book; Horace had too much to drink. I don't drive and it crossed my mind that we might have trouble getting back home with him at the wheel.

He was having a great time, but by the time we got in the car, I knew we were in trouble. Horace started driving and weaving about the streets of San Francisco. As we approached the Bay Bridge, I suggested that perhaps we should park the car and take a cab. Horace wouldn't hear of it.

"Don't worry," he said.

As we entered the ramp, the fender of the car grated along the edge of the curb as Horace kept an unsteady hand on the wheel. I looked ahead and saw huge diesel trucks whizzing by at what appeared to be 100 miles an hour, to say nothing about the multitude of automobiles. I knew we were going to die that night. It was no longer a question of whether we would be hit, but what would hit us first.

To make matters worse, Horace was one of those drivers who looked at you when he talked, no matter what the traffic conditions.

As we drove onto the bridge, weaving all over the white line, the cars and trucks seem to disappear. It may have been because they all spotted a drunk driver ahead, but whatever the reason, he kept on babbling away, mistaking stark terror for rapt attention.

We made it across the bridge, and I knew for sure that Horace was one of those who lived in a state of grace and he was not going before his time.

Horace was a study in deterioration from that time on. It was devastating to watch him come apart. Horace Cayton had been the last of that special breed of Black men in this country who would not compromise their manhood; and I wept as much for an ending of an era as I did for the passing of a great man. The men who would come after him would be told how important it is to be accommodating. Like Malcolm X, Horace did not accommodate. He asked that you take him as he was or not at all. Society allows that kind of freedom in capable White men because it knows the high level of energy and genius that comes from such men. Perhaps when we realize that our most serious energy shortage is from the suppression of this human potential in most non-white people, we can begin to free people to engage in solving problems rather than creating them.

The last time I saw Horace Cayton was on Christmas Eve of 1970. I had done some late Christmas shopping with my KBHK director, Buzz Anderson. Buzz was also from Seattle and knew Horace quite well. We stopped off at the St. Francis Hotel for a drink, and as we came out of the hotel, loaded down with Christmas packages, we saw Horace coming toward us. He wore a jaunty black beret, and was in excellent spirits. He had finally received a grant to finish a literary work started by Richard Wright in Paris, with whom he had been close friends since those early days in Paris, during the 1930's. Wright had been working on a trilogy at the time of his death, but kept the subject matter carefully hidden. Horace invited me to come along as his research assistant if he could get additional money. Even Horace did not know what Wright was writing about, and since he had died unexpectedly, he would have to first see Wright's widow, to gather as much information as possible.

Horace promised to write, and also to send for me, should he get lucky and get additional grant money. Less than one month later Horace Cayton was dead. He died suddenly in his room one night in Paris. I was later shown a letter from a student, written in French and translated by a friend of Horace's, which attempted to piece together the last moments of his life.

Buzz and I attended a memorial for him down at Stanford University Chapel, arranged by his colleague, St. Clair Drake, a visiting Professor there at the time. There I said goodbye to a man who almost single-handedly changed my life.

Horace had given me an inside view of how things function in this society. He had studied it, as a Sociologist, most of his life and easily saw behind the façade that allows people to dream only high enough to serve their masters. He exposed the hidden wheels of fortune that continue to spin for some but not for others. This was his legacy to me: If you arm yourself with knowledge and know where to look, you will begin to see a pattern. It is quite a game—and like it or not—we are all players.

CHAPTER VIII

BREAKING FREE

In 1986, I moved to Honolulu. I have always loved Hawaii. I have relatives there, and I had vacationed there for many years. I felt a change would be good and I might get a chance to pursue a career in television.

I left my family, sold or gave away everything I owned and went to a new place to start all over again. I arrived with eight suitcases—four contained books. I felt like a brand new baby starting all over again.

I wasn't preparing for the end of my life, but a new beginning and different kind of life. Even the spelling of my name changed. When I went down to get my Honolulu I.D. Card, they requested my original birth certificate from the State of California rather than Alameda County. When I received it, it spelled my name Jeraldine (with a "J"). I thought that this was a mistake, but they said my original birth certificate spelled it with a "J". What a thing to discover after all these years. I remember my mother had given birth to all her children at home, and my Aunt Mae had named all of us. Back in the 1920's, a "G" was written just like a "J", so at the county level, someone wrote the "J" as a "G", and no one picked it up. It was a common error.

I, however, found it all very significant to my new life. I have been spelling my name "Jeraldine" or "Jerri" ever since.

After a brief respite on the beaches of Waikiki, I landed a job as a librarian at Kansai Gadai, a Japanese college in 1987. I was host mother to three students. One of them, Takami Yoshie, stayed in touch and has hosted my two trips to Japan.

After six months, I accepted a position at KHET, the public broadcasting station of Hawaii. It was a small, friendly station, and I quickly made friends with the people there. The mood and pace of television is less hectic than in the Bay Area, and I soon found it to be a different working environment.

I was initially hired to research a ten-part series on the subject of leisure called Leisure, which would explore the many ways people will have to deal with leisure time in a world where computers would soon replace workers. I found that almost every advanced country was dealing with this phenomenon except the United States. No corporation wanted to be the one to tell people there would be no jobs in the 21st century, so we could not get funding. The program is still waiting to be done.

I wrote and produced several segments for **Spectrum Hawaii**, a weekly program on the many faceted cultures of Hawaii. It was a fun show to do, and I found myself happy to be in television again. The last program I did was to host a thirteen-part series for Gov. John Waihee, on aging called, *Let's Take Charge,* and funded by the Governor's Commission on Aging. The program visited hospitals, nursing facilities and homes where caregivers took care of the elderly. It also showed many active people in their older years, and how their lifestyles kept them healthy and alive. The station had a wonderful educational department that broadcast to all the other islands, as a supplement to the school program. I was given the opportunity to learn writing and producing, as well as access to all of the technical facilities I was not allowed to touch on the Mainland.

I also hosted a weekly program—*Spectrum Hawaii*—that explored the many facets and multi-cultural richness of Hawaii's diverse population. It also took an in-depth look at the Arts, social and environmental programs throughout the Islands. I produced a segment on the long, rich history of The Royal Hawaiian Hotel. During World War II, it was closed to the public in order to accommodate thousands of military servicemen, for R&R—Rest and Relaxation— from combat. It became an oasis in the middle of the Pacific where exhausted soldiers, sailors and Marines, could recover.

Jerri

On the weekends, the beach was the perfect place to rest and relax. My friends were Asian, Hawaiian, Black and White. We had interesting discussions about race, social upheaval and how Hawaii differed from the Mainland. The Hawaiians were pursuing their rights to their homeland, and were extremely active. Much of their activity did not get publicized for fear it would jeopardize tourism. There are still very active indigenous political movements throughout the islands, and the rest of the South Pacific, including Australia's aboriginal people.

The beauty and ambiance of the islands is also a place to look back on your life and career, particularly the battles you chose to fight. I can say with all my heart that I have never regretted the battles I fought against a television industry that has not lived up to its potential as a teacher and guiding light to humanity. When I think of Marshall McLuhan, Edward R. Murrow, Fred Friendly, and all of those broadcasting pioneers who had such high hopes for this medium, I suddenly feel their pain as I watch what comes out over the airwaves today: Talk shows where participants engage in all types of behavior and subject matter that is questionable, scheduled during the afternoon when children are watching; the continued use of violence to solve problems, sending young people the wrong message. Now, the "reality shows" are taking away what dignity we have left. In the early years, few people understood the power of the medium and what it could do to the fabric of a nation. Now, in my lifetime, I have seen it sink to depths to which even I could never have imagined. I no longer have to sound a clarion call. That call has now gone forth from Congress, and from parents, teachers, students and churches everywhere. And still the madness goes on.

I have even lived long enough to see the media directly influence a presidential election by calling the winner early, before the polls closed, then make a second erroneous call, causing probably millions of people to stay at home and not vote. Then it diverted attention to Florida voting machines and "chads." Whatever number of votes were illegally handled in those precincts, were minute compared to the number of invisible votes we can never tally because they influenced millions of voters we can never trace. That is the power of this medium.

151

That same invisible force dictates behavior, as Vance Packard so chillingly pointed out in his 1950's book, *The Hidden Persuaders*, where he noted that advertisers were paying millions of dollars to behavioral scientists to find out how to get inside people's minds to influence them to buy their products. Packard noted that when carried to the next level it would be the beginning of manipulation and mind control. When people say you can "just turn off your television set", just remember that the perpetrators of drive-by shootings, participants of violence in the schools, workplace and on the streets, are still looking at it.

In the end, the most important things in my life are my children. All of their small insignificant activities as children enriched my life beyond measure. Whatever sacrifices I made pale when I watch them grow into the fine young men they have become. They have passed their tests in life, one by one; they have learned how to fly.

My years in Honolulu were years of growth. To be able to see the ocean and sand every day on the way to work has its own rewards. The air is clean, beauty abounds, and flowers peek out at you from everywhere. There are the same problems in Honolulu that plague every major city, but it is different. There is a spirit that surrounds the islands and protects them from the technological madness that exists elsewhere. It is because the indigenous people of Hawaii will not let it happen. There is a return to their values, love of the land and spiritual ways of the Kahuna—their religion. When I hear them speak, they sound like my father, when he told me so long ago about the ways of the Indian people, how we are one with Mother earth, and should treat it like the Woman it is. There is a time to plant seeds and a time to reap the harvest.

My harvest has come; the seed planted so long ago that I searched for all my life, I have finally found. It was me. I have launched into inner space, and come to understand that to bring order and peace into the world, we must first find it within ourselves. I now understand that my "enemies" are necessary to take me where I must go. Kicking and screaming along the way may help—turning back does not. One must go to a quiet place to go within, meditate and think it through. I was in the best kind of environment to reach back into the past and reflect on my life, while I contemplated the future. The Present was in Paradise and I had enjoyed every minute of it.

I began to learn some of the practices of the Kahuna Priests, and as I waded in the beautiful ocean, I forgave myself for all those I had sinned against and forgave all those who had sinned against me. It was a healing and freeing experience. In a sense I did as Jesus commanded, and "washed my sins away." It was exhilarating!

As I lay on the beach and watched the ocean roll towards the sand, I began to count the waves. Never deviating, constant and steady, beating a path forward, rushing to its destiny, covering the sand with its entire being. Moving powerfully in—and gently out-like two lovers— unashamed, as all the world could see. No earthly power, no war or rumors of war, not hate nor corruption could stop the motion. Just the transcending power of love. We allow the world to complicate our lives when it is all so simple: love and be loved.

For five long years I took time to smell the roses and gardenias; made fresh ginger leis; my eyes drank in the raw beauty of nature in all its glory. It rested my soul. God had been good to me.

*   *   *

After five years I decided to go home. I wanted to publish this memoir I started writing back in 1984, high on top a mountain in a little town called Kula, 3,000 feet up Mt. Haleakala on the island of Maui. That was long ago, and now I needed to get back to family and friends. So I threw a goodbye party, packed up my belongings and flew back to the Mainland. I moved back to Oakland only a short distance from where I was born. I had come full circle, and it had been a great ride. Now I could start anew. I have been involved in many community projects, and most importantly finishing this book. I returned home in 1990 and have watched the new millennium arrive, and wonder if we have learned anything in the process. When I think back on what my life has meant, I remembered the brief time I spent with Professor Arnold Toynbee, the world's greatest living Historian, when I told him my final goal was to become the best human being I could be, then go around the world searching for others. I recalled his unexpected reply: "Well, Jerri, that's the answer after all, isn't it?"

Yes, Professor Toynbee, it is.

*   *   *

Perhaps I can end this book with a poem by Dom Helder Camara, a priest who toiled among the outcasts in the poorest sections of Brazil. His book of poetry is entitled:

A Thousand Reasons For Living.

> Pilgrim:
> when your ship,
> long moored in harbour,
> gives you the illusion
> of being a house;
> when your ship
> begins to put down roots
> in the stagnant water by the quay;
> put out to sea!
> Save your boat's journeying soul
> and your own pilgrim soul,
> cost what it may.

EPILOGUE

Although this book began back in 1984 on a mountaintop on the island of Maui in Hawaii, the events of September 11, 2001, make it imperative to say something about how far we have come, yet how far we have to go. The destruction of the World Trade Center towers in New York City ushered in a new era of vulnerability never before experienced by Americans.

In April of 2001, I was invited by an African American group of Buddhists in the Bay Area to be the Keynote Speaker at their conference—Africa 2000-HARAMBE. The theme: "Revolutionizing the 'African Spirit' in the 21st Century." Here are some excerpts of that speech:

"All religions have one thing in common: We all share the same planet and it is spinning out of control. I would hope this gathering here today is the beginning of the realization that all lasting change starts at the bottom—not at the top. Freedom rises up—oppression trickles down. Today we welcome HARAMBE—UNITY— Revolutionizing the African Spirit—with song, dance, music and joy!

I hope what I say will give you 'pause' to look at our old religions, with new eyes. The Crusades, witch hunts, tribal warfare, ethnic cleansing and that ongoing battle we call the 'Middle East'—are all code words for religious wars. Religion has been used against us— rather than to bring us together. But we all agree on one thing: There is a lot of unlimited power out there—if we can only learn how to use it—and there will never be any rolling blackouts. We all perceive that power in different ways. We are finite beings trying to understand infinite reality. For thousands of years we have had the luxury of expanding and contracting, defining and narrowing, tossing about and re-creating—a whole host of ideas. To Be or Not To Be: that was the question. Well, we have just reached the Millenium and we have run out of time. We no longer have the luxury of arguing over who is right and who is wrong. We must now come together in Love and agree on what is important. In short: FORGET THE LABELS and REMEMBER THE LOVE.

In that spirit, back in the 1970's, two men came together to start a dialogue and wrote a book. The two men were Arnold Toynbee and Daisaku Ikeda, head of Soka Gakkai Buddhist organization. The book was entitled *The Toynbee-Ikeda Dialogue—Man Himself Must Choose.* East met West and the results were startling.

I had the privilege of meeting Arnold Toynbee back in 1972 on a trip to London. I had written a speech entitled **Blacks in Broadcasting** and sent it to him, requesting an interview. To my surprise he called and asked me to come the next day.

I later found out it was because we were writing about the same thing. My speech said, in part: 'We have built a technology machine that requires us to go to other lands, rich in natural resources, in order to feed it. We justify our presence there by "liberating" the people from a fate worse than death—self-determination. As the machine grows bigger, it dehumanizes us, and we stand before it, powerless. This machine has become so complex that it has also caused us to pollute our environment. Through ignorance and greed, the air has been rendered unfit to breath, water unfit to drink, and food unfit to eat. We are in trouble all over the world, and on the brink of disaster at home.

What kind of man destroys the thing that gives him life? And creates a crisis which threatens our very existence as a species on this planet?"

Being on the same wavelength brought about the interview and I spent a memorable two hours with the world's greatest living historian. He had made a long trip to Japan after the war and was studying their culture. The result was the book. They discussed many things: politics, war, Man as a social being, good and evil, health and welfare, and the nature of things. But they also discussed religion and this is what they had to say:

"IKEDA: I sense one common point distinguishing the new religions—faith in scientific progress, nationalism, and communism—from such older ones as Christianity, Buddhism, and Islam. Whereas the older religions strove to control and suppress human greed, the newer ones seem to have originated—or at least to be employed—for the sake of the liberation and fulfillment of that greed. I consider this to be the basic nature of the new religions, and in that nature I see the fundamental problem facing all three of them.

TOYNBEE: I think you are correct, consequently, I feel the need for a new kind of religion. Mankind has been united, socially, for the first time in history, by the worldwide spread of modern civilization. The question of mankind's future religion arises because all the current religions have proved unsatisfactory.

The future religion need not necessarily be an entirely new religion. It might be a new version of one of the old religions . . . A future religion that is to bring into being, and to keep in being, a new civilization, will have to be one that will enable mankind to contend with and to overcome, the evils that are serious present threats to human survival. The most formidable of these evils are the oldest: greed, which is as old as life itself is, and war and social injustice, which are as old as civilization. A new evil that is hardly less formidable is the artificial environment that mankind has created through the application of science to technology in the service of greed.

IKEDA: My thinking on this topic is in complete agreement with yours. I, too, consider the major evils besetting our civilization to be greed, which is inherent in life itself; war and injustice, which are—as you say—as old as civilization; and the artificial destruction of the natural environment. Greed is a matter between the individual human being and himself; war and injustice are ills between human beings on the social plane, and environmental destruction involves relationships between man and nature . . .

To effect any kind of improvement in the world situation, each individual must improve—indeed revolutionize—himself from within.

That is, we must take steps to set the first set of relations in order. Then and only then is it possible to do something about the upsets in our social organization and in the natural environment."

* * *

That was the dialogue between East and West.

So it seems—we're all on the same page:

1) How can we bring all of the religions together to fight a common enemy: Greed?
2) How can we ensure that the needs of humanity keep equal pace with the advance of technology?
3) How do we revolutionize the African Spirit in the 21st Century?

Toynbee and Ikeda went straight to the heart of the matter: We must begin with ourselves—the individual. You are the key to the solution. We have seen our institutions fail, one by one. They can not even keep the lights on any more. What a metaphor! We are being kept in the dark by the most powerful nation on earth!

It is time to turn on our own personal electricity. Turn on the light inside you and light up the world. We once we had that power—and we can have it again. All we have to do is plug in. Just like your radio, television, or telephone . . . all forms of communication. You are the vehicle awaiting the flow of electricity—the ultimate form of communication—ready to go. We have all been so distracted by movies, television and all those irrelevant things outside ourselves—created to grab our attention, that we have failed to pay attention. Do an about face, turn around and take a good look at yourself. You are waiting to get plugged in, and when the power goes on inside—there will be no stopping us. Because while the rest of the world is turning out their lights, we'll be turning ours on! That is real communication, turning on the electricity . . . and no one can turn it off but you. We just have to decide when to do it.

If we can all come together in unity—we won't have to grapple with whether or not there is an apology for slavery, or justice to the

American Indian. It will take place naturally. Nor will we watch the continuous rape of our natural resources. Our children will no longer feel the rage that causes them to pack guns instead of books to school. Our love and respect for nature and ourselves will begin to replace the damage that has been inflicted on this beautiful, once tranquil, round, fertile, loving Being, called Earth.

ACKNOWLEDGMENTS

First, I thank the Creator for being a constant presence in my life. Without that constant feeling of Love and Acceptance in my life, I could not have written this book.

My deepest gratitude to my publisher, Ishmael Reed, for his faith in this book and for believing in me since the very beginning. Thanks also to Malcolm Kelly for his excellent suggestions that helped pull the story together. Sincere thanks to Dr. Barbara Cannon for her constant friendship and for her careful reading and refining of the manuscript. My gratitude to Dr. Shirley Thornton for her support for my first book on media, and for her continued interest in my work in the Media. I would also like to thank Susan Robinson for her intuitive suggestions and intelligent choices in typing this manuscript. My gratitude to Karla Brundage whose first-rate editing helped me open up this book in ways I could never have imagined. Thanks also to Julian and Dr. Raye Richardson and their son, Billy Richardson, for printing my first self-published book, *The Power, Magic and Imagination of Media*, a series of speeches I gave while in the television business. Two speeches appear in this book. Also special thanks to Ernest Crutchfield, former President of Laney College, for assisting me and supporting my efforts to distribute the first book. Thanks to Carole Ward Allen, Prof. of Women's Studies at Laney College for her continued support in setting up readings of my manuscript to her classes. To my many supporters along the way, who have stuck by me and always encouraged my efforts: Dr. Doris Ward, Geoffrey Pete, Noble Fields, Rev. Roland Gordon, Tim and Tamsen Horan (who

sponsored my first book signing of the Media book at their Holmes
Bookstore), Joe and Loretta Johnson, Ida Jackson, Ruth Acty, Florence
Jury, Leone Baxter Whitaker, Liang Ho and Rev. Earl Horn. Thanks to
Maria Theresa Caen for valuable editing of my earlier manuscript. My
sincere gratitude to Dianna Miller for arranging a reading of the
manuscript at Mills College. My deep appreciation to Zakiya Zendayi
of Laney College and Rev. Robert McKnight, of Merritt College for
allowing me to read from my manuscript in their African American
Studies Classes.

Thanks to Jerry Thompson, Public Relations Manager for Barnes
and Noble, for his guidance and suggestions on the manuscript, and
to Mickey Mayzes, for her constant assistance and media expertise.
Thanks also to Jimmy Guy and Ed Broussard for keeping community
television programming alive, and discussions of my books on the air.

My indebtedness to the late Scott Newhall, who took time out of
his busy schedule to write a beautiful Introduction to this
autobiography. Scotty, his wife Ruth, and their son, Tony, have been
warm and gracious friends to me. Deep gratitude to Dr. Eugene
Whitworth for his lovely Preface to this book. He and his lovely wife,
Ruth have been great anchors during the storm.

To Dr. Stuart Hyde, who arranged for me to become a writer-in-
residence at Montalvo in Saratoga, to finish a difficult chapter in this
book, my thanks.

To Mark Canosio, a student in my BCA class at San Francisco State
University, who encouraged me in a letter to write this book. Mark has
passed away, so I give my thanks to his father Dino Canosio.

To Bob Yamada, of the Berkeley Historical Society for his reading
of the manuscript and insightful suggestions.

To Dr. James Daly, Diablo Valley College, for sharing of ideas and
support.

To Ted Kurihara, who started photographing me during my early
days of television and graciously continued to assist me in my
community activities.

To my friends of long standing, school chums from yesteryear, up
to my new friends in the Bay Area and Honolulu . . . my warmest and
sincere gratitude for all of your support and friendship. To Rhonda

Jones, thanks for connecting me with the At-risk teenagers of Oakland and helping me understand their problems. I am indebted to my old and new friends in the Bay Area and Honolulu for their on-going support and friendship. Warmest thanks to Coralee Callins, Glora and Gus Jacobs, Peaches & Hank Boulden, Sheila Kilgore, Betty and Sam Golden, Candy Gayles, Herman Wiggan, and L.M. Johnson of "The Californians", for helping me remember what it was like growing up in Oakland and Berkeley.

My warm thanks and appreciation to Teola Sanders, founder of "Today's Women", in Oakland and Sharon Yarbrough founder of "Sister 2 Sister" in Honolulu, for their support in arranging discussion of my books and for bringing together African American women to better serve the community. To Jennifer King, Director of the West Oakland Senior Center and her Administrative Assistant, Janie Daniels, for their kindness and patience in guiding me through the uncertain mysteries of the Computer, enabling me to finish my book across the street from DeFremery Park, where I played as a child.

To my beloved family: My mother and father, Laura and Turner Wilson. Without their unconditional love I could not have come this far. To my sisters, Lorraine (deceased) and Phyllis and brother Stan, my cousins Hazel Linyard and Vernadine (Plucky) Perry for providing me with a family unit in which to grow. My extended family of cousins, nephews, nieces, for being there for me when it counted. To my nephew Paul Wilson for transferring important information on computer discs. To my nephew Steve Striplin for working so hard on the Family Reunion, along with my nieces, Leslie, Michelle and Luana. Most of all, my love to my three sons, Ted, Michael and James, without whose support and encouragement this book would never have been written. And to the future of our family—my grandsons, Ted IV and Turner, for making me proud.

ABOUT THE AUTHOR

Jerri Lange has had a wealth of experience in television (both in front of the cameras and behind the scenes.) Between 1969 and 1979, she was host of a number of television programs which focused on community issues at KEMO, KBHK, KGO and KQED (where she also served on the Board.) Her colorful career yielded numerous awards in the field of broadcasting.

As a professor of Broadcast Communication Arts at San Francisco State University, she taught Broadcasting and Affirmative Action, Women in Media, and Writing for Radio and Television. She also lectured a graduate class in Communications at Stanford University. She was granted an interview with Professor Arnold Toynbee, historian and member of the Royal Institute of International Studies in London. Her credits also include special correspondent in Africa for the *San Francisco Chronicle,* where she worked for three years as an editorial secretary. After turning her talents to public relations consulting, and editing and publishing a magazine, she left California for Honolulu, Hawaii, where she became writer, producer and host at KHET-TV. She also published, designed and created a unique multicultural magazine entitled *Amberstar* in 1985, celebrating and valuing diversity, a common thread throughout Jerri's life.

She lives in Oakland, California.